THE
FRESH & GREEN
TABLE

THE FRESH & GREEN TABLE

Delicious Ideas for Bringing Vegetables Into Every Meal

BY SUSIE MIDDLETON
AUTHOR OF *Fast, Fresh & Green*

Photographs by ANNABELLE BREAKEY

CHRONICLE BOOKS
SAN FRANCISCO

For Roy and Libby

Library of Congress Cataloging-in-Publication Data available.
ISBN: 978-1-4521-0265-8

Manufactured in China

Designed by Lynda Lucas
Production Assistance by DC Typography
Typeset in Avenir, **Beton** & **Archive Kludsky**

Food styling by Karen Shinto
Prop styling by Emma Star Jensen
Food styling assistance by Jeffrey Larsen

10 9 8 7 6 5 4 3 2

Chronicle Books LLC
680 Second Street
San Francisco, California 94107
www.chroniclebooks.com

CONTENTS

Introduction: Moving Veggies to the Center of the Plate

I remember the thrill of the first time—the first time I grilled a pizza, the first time I hand-shaped a rustic tart, the first time I made a great chili. Funny thing is, I still get a thrill out of learning how to cook something new. For me, cooking is all about technique, and every day I thank my lucky stars for the cooking skills I've collected over the years. I feel so grateful, in fact, that all I really want to do is pass the best of that knowledge on to you. You might think that cooking vegetables is all about the ingredients. (Vegetables are, after all, so sexy.) But I think the real secret to making delicious vegetable dishes is a repertoire of good and easy techniques, brought to life—of course—in detailed recipes.

I'm hoping you and I can use these techniques and recipes to blow vegetable cooking out a bit. Veggies are ready for their day in the limelight—they're not just for vegetarians or vegans, but for all of us. And while veggies are perfectly comfortable hanging out on the side of an entrée, they can move to the center of the plate with amazing agility. I know—I've been a witness!

After writing my first cookbook, *Fast, Fresh & Green*—a collection of vegetable *side* dishes—I began to think about the possibilities of vegetable *main* dishes. Since I'm not a vegetarian, my mind didn't wander to recipes that feature soy or other meat substitutes. Instead I immediately thought about the kinds of dishes that everyone—meat-eaters and vegetarians alike—would already be familiar and comfortable with, things like soups, salads, and stir-fries. Next I thought of pastas and frittatas—dishes that could easily star veggies front and center. Then I considered the fun factor—recipes that are a real kick to make and eat—things like grilled pizza and savory rustic tarts. Boy, would they make great veggie vehicles. Pretty soon my mind went into overdrive: Grains! Gratins! Galettes! Oh My! Suddenly, my list of vegetable main-dish recipes was too long for one book.

So I've narrowed down. A bit. (My editors are breathing a sigh of relief.) But you will find in *The Fresh & Green Table* (and by green we mean all things vegetable, red tomatoes and orange squash included) that I have not skimped on two things: recipes with lots of details—and recipes that yield delicious results. (My very, very favorite, to be completely honest, is the first recipe in this book, Grilled Zucchini, Bell Pepper, Goat Cheese & Grilled Bread Salad with Double-Tomato Vinaigrette, page 12. But there are so many more.)

Why are the recipes so detailed?

In the detailed recipes, you'll find good techniques waiting for you to absorb. Slow down, sit back, and read the recipes through before starting. Pay close attention to things like the type of pan called for, the way the vegetable is cut, and when ingredients are added. But, most especially, pay attention to the "doneness" clues I provide. (How brown is it? Is the pan sizzling? Is the sauce bubbling?) This isn't just me being fussy—it's me doing my best to hand you the tools to becoming a good cook, tools I've picked up from every cooking experience I've ever had—from culinary school to my first restaurant job to my days as editor of *Fine Cooking* magazine. Sensual clues—what something looks like, smells like, sounds like—are more reliable than cooking times. (Rest assured, however, that my cross-testers and I have made every effort to give you the best possible estimates on timing. But every stove is a little different.)

Also, make more than one recipe in a chapter, and you'll begin to see the takeaways. For example, most of the grain dishes in chapter 8 pair a simple cooked grain (like quinoa or farro) with a sautéed or roasted vegetable (like carrots or green beans). Make a couple of these recipes, and soon you'll be improvising your own combos. You'll have a new kind of dish in your repertoire—one defined by the details of the way it's made.

But to be clear, what exactly is a vegetable main dish?

A veggie main dish is any recipe that features vegetables and is substantial and interesting enough to plan a meal around. It doesn't have to be the *entire* meal (though many dishes can be), but it should be a major component. In fact, the primary goal of a veggie main dish is to get you thinking of great ways to eat more veggies and to shift the portions on your plate so that meat might play a supporting role in dinner, rather than a starring one. If you're a vegetarian (in which case meat isn't playing a role at all), you probably already think of veggies in this way. But perhaps now you're looking for veggie main dishes that feel familiar to your non-vegetarian eating companions, so you can all eat veggies together.

Regardless of your world eating view—and I think of mine as pro-veggie, rather than anti-meat—you might enjoy eating a more veggie-centric meal at dinnertime for two other reasons: Veggies are delicious (especially when cooked well), and they're incredibly versatile. (That's where the fun-in-the-kitchen part comes in—a big priority for me.) And, yes, veggies are really good for you; it goes without saying that we'd all like the benefits of eating more of those antioxidants. But since I'm a cook, and not a nutritionist, I can only speak to what I intuitively know best: If something tastes good, people will eat more of it.

How do I begin including these dishes in my meals?

Here's a list of the twenty kinds of main dishes in this book from which you can choose if you're looking for a satisfying destination for your veggies:

1. Warm Salads
2. Grilled Salads
3. Creamy Soups
4. Chunky Soups
5. Chili
6. Stovetop Pastas
7. Baked Pastas
8. Cool Pastas
9. Frittatas
10. Savory Bread Puddings
11. Gratins*
12. *Tians**
13. Galettes*

    **(I'll explain these, I promise!)*

14. Savory Rustic Tarts
15. Veggie Sautés
16. Ragoûts
17. Grain and Veggie Combos
18. Rice and Veggie Combos
19. Baked Pizzas
20. Grilled Pizzas

As I mentioned earlier, many of the recipes, like, say, Orecchiette with Lemony Broccoflower & Toasted Garlic Bread Crumbs (page 58) or Spring Veggie Ragoût with Baby Artichokes, Fingerling Potatoes & Spinach (page 142), are one-dish wonders (a.k.a. complete meals). Others, like Caramelized Winter Veggies with Collard Green "Confetti" (page 133) or Green Bean, Red Onion & Cherry Tomato Ragoût with Pomegranate Pan Sauce (page 138) make a meal when paired with a side dish like polenta (page 210) or rice pilaf (page 208)—or when served with a few slices of roast chicken or pork on the side. And a few, like the Savoy Cabbage, Apple, Onion & Gruyère Rustic Tart (page 118), for example, beg to be eaten in smaller portions and to be paired with a generous green salad or a cup of soup.

To help you wrap your head around how a particular recipe might fit into your meal planning, I've included serving suggestions in the headnotes whenever possible. (And many times, I offer ways of rounding out a meal for both meat-eaters and vegetarians.) Also, I've included a collection of simple and delicious side dishes and side salads in chapter 10 (page 188) so that these perfect accompaniments for veggie main dishes will be right at your fingertips.

What makes a veggie main dish sing?

Here's how my simple mind thinks: Good technique + detailed recipes = great flavor and texture. On my veggie blog, SixBurnerSue.com, I'm always talking about how much I love high-heat cooking methods—roasting, sautéing, and grilling. There's hardly a vegetable that doesn't benefit from the caramelized flavor it picks up when cooked with high heat. So you will find that in many recipes in this book, veggies are cooked first before joining other ingredients in the main dish. In addition to thinking about how I'm going to cook my vegetables, I think about my choice of vegetables. Before I even focus on a primary veggie—say, broccoli or green beans—I think about aromatic veggies as a base for a dish. The best aromatics are all members of the allium family—garlic, shallots, onions, leeks—and browning them as part of the flavor base for a vegetable dish is one trick for making a meatless dish taste meatier. My other favorite aromatic is fresh ginger, which I use in soups, sautés, and even custards.

Next, I think about pairing a "meaty" vegetable (even in small amounts) with a lighter-feeling green vegetable to make a more satisfying main-dish combo. Mushrooms are the meatiest vegetable of all, but eggplant, winter roots, potatoes, fall squashes—even an occasional green vegetable like artichoke hearts—can play this role. Regardless of the veggie combo, I always add flavor boosts like fresh herbs, citrus juices and zests, or fresh pepper at the end of cooking.

For texture, complexity, and satisfaction, proteins and carbs are welcome partners in veggie main dishes. Consider the crispy, smoky contrast of a grilled pizza crust. The flaky, buttery crust of a tart. The pop-in-your-mouth satisfaction of whole grains like wheat berries. The chili-and-quesadilla-comfort of earthy black beans. You get the idea. I even use a little meat as a condiment in some veggie main dishes, as I did in *Fast, Fresh & Green*. However, because I tried hard to keep the majority of the dishes in this book vegetarian-friendly, 90 percent of them are actually meat-free.

Ahem . . . Are these dishes good for you?

Speaking of proteins and meatless diets and buttery crusts . . . I know how hard it is to navigate nutritional advice these days. And I know I've already mentioned that I don't approach vegetable cooking from a nutritionist's point of view, but from that of a cook. But I think it's important for me to share just one more aspect of my world cooking view with you.

I occasionally blog for the Huffington Post. I ostensibly write about potlucks and farmers' markets and vegetable gardening, but really all my blogs are about one thing: Cooking more at home. This is something I feel strongly about; I don't believe that our country's diet woes are caused by too many good home-cooked meals. I don't believe that any whole food—including butter and the much-maligned cheese—is bad for you in moderation. (To paraphrase Julia Child, if you don't eat butter, your hair will fall out.) Eating well at home with our families and friends is not only one of life's biggest pleasures, but also one less meal we eat out. Or to put it this way, it's one more meal where we avoid the large portions, the excess bad stuff (sugar, sodium, preservatives, trans-fats), and the costs (yes) of eating processed or take-out food—the real culprits.

Learning to cook vegetables deliciously means you will eat more of them. Period. It's that simple.

Very few people are going to eat microwaved broccoli every day of the week (or even two nights in a row!). But if you offer Broccoli & Cheddar Frittata with Red Potatoes & Scallions (page 86); Southwestern Spiced Butternut Squash & Apple Soup with Lime, Cilantro & Yogurt (page 34); Greek Spinach-Salad Pasta with Feta, Olives, Artichokes, Tomatoes & Pepperoncini (page 67); Warm Winter Salad of Roasted Root "Fries" with Shallot and Sherry-Maple Vinaigrette (page 23); and Broccoli Raab, Sausage, Goat Cheese & Sun-Dried Tomato Pizza (page 177) five nights in a row, who's eating more vegetables now?!

I know—that may seem like a fantasy scenario. And I'm not suggesting you go from zero to one hundred in a week. Realistically, I'm just hoping that *The Fresh & Green Table* can offer you the opportunity for more freedom, more creativity, more deliciousness—with vegetables, with dinner, and with your cooking. I know cooking from scratch takes time, but I also know you bought this book because you think it's time worth taking. Hurrah!

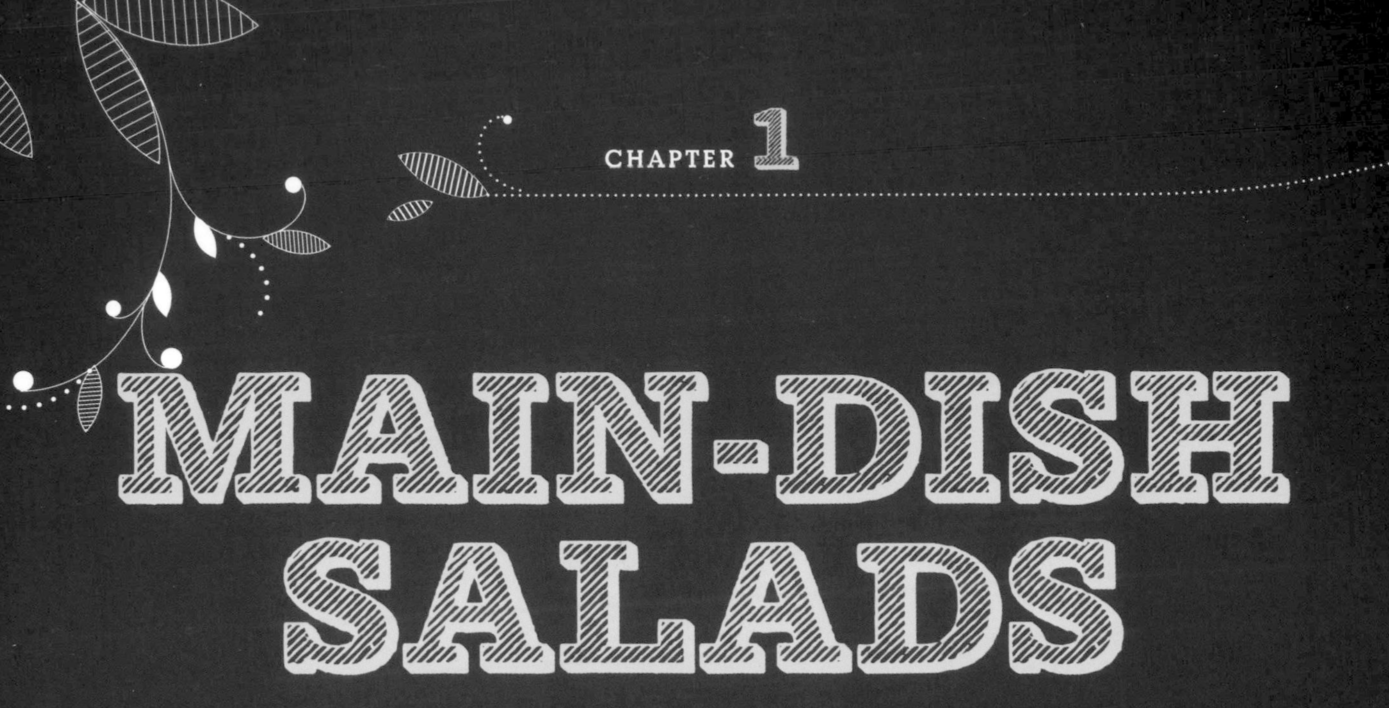

CHAPTER 1

MAIN-DISH SALADS

Summer Salads

Winter Salads

Making A Main-Dish Salad: **How It Works**

It's no accident that main-dish salads are the first chapter in this book. Salad cheerleader that I am (Go arugula! Go escarole!), I couldn't be happier with the trend in recent years to put salad at the center of the dinner plate. When you think "fresh and green for dinner," of course you think salad first! But the truth is, there are good main-dish salads and bad main-dish salads. Bad ones have wilty greens, drab dressings, and lackluster ingredients. Fortunately, it's easy to banish these culprits and elevate the salad (and the vegetables) on your dinner plate to star status.

About those greens. Ironically, the wider availability of groovy prewashed salad mixes has made it easy for us to cut corners when it comes to making good salads. Salad mixes have problems, though: They rot quickly and often feature delicate greens that don't hold up to warm ingredients. If you really want a great main-dish salad, make your own salad mix—with at least one variety of sturdy lettuce in it. (Heads of lettuce are fresher than mixes, too.)

In winter, start your mix with escarole or frisée; in warmer months, start with Boston or Bibb. Romaine (or its cousin, cos) is a good base for any season. Nothin' wrong with adding a bit of bagged baby arugula or spinach (you know what you're getting). Then round out the mix with a small amount of slivered radicchio, endive, or napa cabbage for crunch and color. (To save time, prep greens ahead, see page 189).

And the problem of drab dressings? Easily solved by making your own vinaigrette. A vinaigrette in its simplest form is just three parts oil to one part acid. A pinch of salt or a dab of mustard helps the oil and vinegar to emulsify. But there are endless tricks (fresh garlic or ginger, citrus zest, salty capers and olives, fresh herbs) you can use to zip up a vinaigrette. You'll find great examples in all the recipes in this chapter (and in the lovely side salads on pages 191 to 195, too). Please avoid bottled salad dressings, which contain corn syrup, MSG, or any number of processed ingredients.

Now to the good stuff. A main-dish salad needs hearty, filling ingredients. So for a moment, forget cucumbers, radishes, and bean sprouts. Think grilled portobellos and asparagus, roasted sweet potatoes and parsnips, crispy red potatoes, and caramelized beets. Not only are these veggies hearty, but you'll notice they're all grilled, roasted, or sautéed. High-heat cooking infuses the veggies with a sweetness and depth of flavor that's both salad-friendly and dinner-worthy. So by using one of these methods to cook your salad veggies, you're taking a huge step toward main-dish deliciousness.

Finally, don't forget to add interest and texture with toasted nuts, flavorful cheeses, Rustic Croutons (page 199), or Grilled Bread (page 203). And know that while veggies star in these salads, it's easy enough to tuck a few grilled shrimp or a couple of slices of seared steak amid the greenery, too.

Grilled Zucchini, Bell Pepper, Goat Cheese & Grilled Bread Salad

with Double-Tomato Dressing

{Summer Salads} I know I'm not supposed to play favorites. So let me just say I'm awfully fond of this vibrant, colorful, fun-to-assemble, delicious taste of summer. It bursts with flavor, starting with a layer of grilled bread, followed by grilled zucchini, goat cheese, grill-roasted red peppers, lots of fresh herbs, and a tomato vinaigrette with both cherry tomatoes and sun-dried tomatoes. The recipe was inspired by a side dish I developed for *Fast, Fresh & Green* in which I paired warm goat cheese with the caramelized flavor of grill-roasted bell peppers. I knew that such a combo would make an even better main dish with grilled bread, grilled zucchini, and the fabulous tomato dressing. You'll have fun prepping this, but it takes a bit of time. Since it's a great dish to serve to friends, I suggest prepping most of the ingredients a few hours ahead and then grilling and assembling when friends arrive. (You can grill the peppers ahead, but wait on the zucchini and bread.) Have fun stacking the layers, and make the salad look pretty in your own way; just be sure to distribute the good stuff evenly among the four portions.

SERVES 4

→

2 large RED BELL PEPPERS, about 7 oz/200 g each (choose long peppers over blocky ones)

2 large ZUCCHINI (10 to 11 oz/ 280 to 310 g each)

⅓ cup/75 ml EXTRA-VIRGIN OLIVE OIL

KOSHER SALT

Four ½-in-/12-mm-thick PEASANT BREAD (from a boule or other large loaf— slices should be oval, about 7 in/17 cm long and 3 or 4 in/7.5 to 10 cm wide)

1 large GARLIC CLOVE, peeled and halved

3 cups/55 g BABY ARUGULA LEAVES

¼ cup/10 g very roughly chopped BASIL and MINT LEAVES

4 oz/115 g FRESH GOAT CHEESE (crumbled while still cold), at room temperature or slightly warmed

DOUBLE-TOMATO DRESSING (recipe follows)

1 ***Heat a gas grill to high.*** While the grill is heating, put the whole bell peppers directly on the grate, close the lid, and cook, turning every couple of minutes, until the peppers are well blistered and blackened in most places, 10 to 12 minutes. (They do not need to be completely blackened, or the skin will stick.) Transfer the peppers to a bowl and cover tightly with aluminum foil. Let sit for 10 to 20 minutes. Over a fine-mesh strainer placed over a bowl (to catch juices), peel the skin away from the peppers; it should come right off. (Reserve any accumulated juices.) Put the peppers on a cutting board and split them lengthwise along the lobes. Gently remove and discard the seeds, but *do not* rinse the peppers. You will probably wind up with six or seven long pieces (total from both peppers). You will need eight long pieces total, so split two pieces in half lengthwise again. (They will be skinnier pieces, which is fine; you can use them as the top layer.)

2 ***Reduce the grill heat to medium.*** Trim the ends from the zucchini and halve them crosswise (not lengthwise!). You will now have four pieces, each about 3 to 4 in/7.5 to 10 cm long. Stand one piece on end on your cutting board. Trim a sliver from two sides of each piece (to avoid having pieces with a lot of skin), and then cut down through the zucchini at ¼-in/6-mm intervals to yield four or five slices or "planks" per zucchini half. Do the same with the remaining pieces. You'll have a total of 16 to 20 pieces. Arrange the pieces in a single layer on a foil-lined baking sheet and brush them generously on both sides with about 2½ tbsp of the olive oil and season them with a little salt.

3 ***Generously brush the bread slices*** on both sides with the remaining olive oil and sprinkle them with a little salt.

4 ***Arrange the bread slices*** and the zucchini pieces in a single layer on the grill and close the lid. Grill the bread until golden brown on both sides, 1 to 2 minutes per side. Cook the zucchini until well marked on the first side, 3 to 5 minutes. Flip and cook on the other side until marked, 2 to 3 minutes more. (Transfer the zucchini to a tray or plate and cover loosely with foil to retain heat.) Rub the grilled bread on both sides with the cut sides of the garlic.

5 ***Set aside a few arugula leaves*** for garnish and divide the remaining leaves evenly among four plates, scattering them loosely. Sprinkle about one-third of the herbs over the arugula. Place a bread slice in the center of each plate. Drizzle the bread with any accumulated pepper juices (if you have any). Begin layering by topping each bread slice with two pieces of grilled zucchini, placing them on a slight diagonal. Sprinkle half of the goat cheese over the zucchini. Cover the goat cheese with a piece of roasted pepper, using the larger pieces on this layer, and again placing them on a slight diagonal. Top the roasted pepper with another third of the herbs and then with the remaining goat cheese. Top the goat cheese with two more pieces of zucchini and the remaining herbs. Then top each serving with the last piece of roasted pepper. Spoon an equal amount of the dressing around and over each of the "sandwiches" and top with a few leaves of the reserved arugula. Serve right away.

Double-Tomato Dressing

4 tbsp/60 ml EXTRA-VIRGIN OLIVE OIL

2 tbsp finely chopped, drained, OIL-PACKED SUN-DRIED TOMATOES

1 tbsp plus 1 tsp RED WINE VINEGAR

1 tbsp ORANGE JUICE

1 tbsp combination of finely chopped FRESH MINT and BASIL

1 tsp HONEY

½ tsp good quality BLACK-OLIVE TAPENADE

½ tsp minced GARLIC

¼ tsp KOSHER SALT

6 oz/170 g small CHERRY TOMATOES or OTHER TINY TOMATOES, halved or quartered, depending on size

In a small bowl, whisk together all the ingredients except the fresh tomatoes until well combined. Gently fold in the tomatoes. Let sit at room temperature while you prepare the salad. Stir gently before serving. **MAKES 1¼ CUPS/300 ML**

Nine-Layer Grilled Vegetable Salad

with Avocados, Black Beans & Lemon-Cilantro Vinaigrette

FOR THE GRILL

2 medium ears **FRESH CORN**, shucked

1 large **RED ONION** (8 oz/225 g)

1 medium-large **ZUCCHINI** (8 to 10 oz/225 to 280 g)

¼ cup/60 ml **EXTRA-VIRGIN OLIVE OIL**

KOSHER SALT

1 large **RED** or **YELLOW BELL PEPPER** (8 to 9 oz/225 to 255 g)

FOR THE VINAIGRETTE

6 tbsp/90 ml **EXTRA-VIRGIN OLIVE OIL**

2 tbsp freshly squeezed **LEMON JUICE**

½ tsp finely grated **LEMON ZEST**

1 tsp **HONEY**

2 tbsp chopped **FRESH CILANTRO**

½ tsp minced **GARLIC**

⅛ tsp **GROUND CUMIN**

⅛ tsp **GROUND CORIANDER**

KOSHER SALT

FRESHLY GROUND PEPPER

{Summer Salads} There's so much to like about this salad, with its layers of smoky grilled veggies, crisp lettuce, creamy avocado, tangy goat cheese, "meaty" black beans, and crunchy nuts. For a pretty presentation, assemble the salad in a glass bowl. But here's the thing: It does get tumbled up when dressed and tossed, and it winds up looking a bit rustic (but tasting fabulous nevertheless). To keep it smart looking at a picnic or potluck, don't dress and toss it until you're ready to serve. Or, if you're having the boss over, arrange the salad on individual plates or in shallow bowls and then drizzle the vinaigrette over it. You can grill the vegetables an hour or two ahead (they don't need to be hot) and make the vinaigrette ahead to space out the prep on this. Grilled Bread (page 203) would be a nice side for this satisfying salad.

SERVES 4

1 ***To grill the vegetables:*** Bring a large saucepan of water to a boil. Drop in the corn, cover, and turn off the heat. Let sit for 5 minutes and then drain.

2 ***Trim the ends from the red onion*** and cut it crosswise into ½-in-/12-mm-thick rings. (Remove the peel.) You should get five or six rings. Place the rings (keeping them together) in a single layer on a large baking sheet. Trim the ends from the zucchini and halve it crosswise so that you have two pieces that are each about 4 in/10 cm long. Stand one piece on its end. Trim a sliver from two sides (to avoid pieces with a lot of skin) and then cut down through the zucchini at ¼-in/6-mm intervals to yield four or five slices or "planks" per zucchini half. Do the same with the remaining half. You should have about ten planks. Arrange the zucchini and the corn in a single layer on the baking sheet. Brush the zucchini, corn, and onion generously on all sides with the olive oil (you may not use it all) and season them with salt.

3 ***Heat a gas grill to high.*** While the grill is heating, put the whole bell pepper directly on the grate and close the lid. Grill the pepper until blistered but not entirely blackened, turning it every couple of minutes, for a total of 10 to 12 minutes. Transfer the pepper to a plate or bowl and cover tightly with aluminum foil. Let sit while you grill the other vegetables.

FOR THE SALAD

One 15½-oz/445-g can BLACK BEANS, drained

6 cups (11 oz/310 g) chopped ROMAINE LETTUCE

2 ripe medium AVOCADOS, cut into ½-in/12-mm dice and tossed with a little olive oil

Kosher salt

1 cup (4 oz/115 g) cold GOAT CHEESE, crumbled while still chilled

⅓ cup/35 g TOASTED SLIVERED ALMONDS (see page 198)

4 ***Reduce the grill heat to medium.*** Arrange the corn, onion rings (keeping the rings together as best you can), and zucchini slices in a single layer on the grill, close the lid, and cook, covered, until the vegetables are nicely marked on the bottom sides, 2 to 3 minutes for the corn, 4 minutes for zucchini, and 5 to 6 minutes for the onion. (If desired, give the zucchini and onion a half-turn halfway through cooking the first side to make crosshatch marks.)

5 ***Turn the corn to another side*** and turn the onion and zucchini over. Close the lid and grill until well marked on the other side, another 2 to 3 minutes for the corn, 2 to 3 minutes for the zucchini, and 5 to 6 minutes for the onion. Turn the corn one or two more times until it is somewhat brown on all sides, another 2 to 4 minutes. Transfer the zucchini and the grilled corn to plates to cool. Transfer the onion to a plate and cover with foil. Let the onion sit for 5 to 10 minutes so that it will steam to finish cooking and become tender.

6 ***Cut the kernels from the corncobs.*** Peel and seed the bell pepper and cut it into 3/4-in/2-cm pieces. Cut the zucchini into 3/4-in/2-cm pieces. Coarsely chop the red onion.

7 ***To make the vinaigrette:*** In a small bowl, combine the olive oil, lemon juice, lemon zest, honey, cilantro, garlic, cumin, coriander, a big pinch of salt, and several grinds of pepper. Whisk until well combined.

8 ***To make the salad:*** In a small bowl, toss the black beans in 1 tbsp of the vinaigrette. Put the lettuce in a large salad bowl. Top the lettuce with the avocados and sprinkle it with a little salt. In successive layers, add the roasted peppers, black beans, corn, red onion, zucchini, goat cheese, and toasted almonds.

9 ***Drizzle with 4 to 5 tbsp/60 to 75 ml of the vinaigrette*** and toss very gently with salad utensils or two serving spoons (not tongs) to combine everything. Taste and dress with more vinaigrette, if needed before serving. (Alternatively, divide the lettuce evenly among four dinner plates or four large shallow bowls and arrange one-quarter of each of the salad ingredients in layers in each. Drizzle about a generous 1 tbsp of vinaigrette over each salad and pass the remainder.)

Grilled Potato, Shrimp, Green Bean & Summer Tomato Salad

FOR THE VINAIGRETTE

3/4 cup/180 ml EXTRA-VIRGIN OLIVE OIL

3 tbsp plus 1 tsp WHITE BALSAMIC VINEGAR

1 tbsp plus 1 tsp freshly squeezed LEMON JUICE

1/2 tsp minced GARLIC

1/2 tsp minced ANCHOVY (about 1 anchovy)

1/4 tsp DIJON MUSTARD

1/4 tsp KOSHER SALT

Dash of WORCESTERSHIRE SAUCE

FRESHLY GROUND PEPPER

FOR THE SALAD

16 BABY RED POTATOES of uniform size (about 1 1/4 to 1 1/2 oz/35 to 40 g each)

KOSHER SALT

1/2 lb/225 g GREEN BEANS, trimmed

3 tbsp MAYONNAISE

1 tbsp DIJON MUSTARD

20 large SHRIMP (21–25 count), peeled and deveined

FRESHLY GROUND PEPPER

6 oz/170 g BIBB or BOSTON LETTUCE, torn into small pieces

{Summer Salads} A salad for everyone, this is fresh and filling and rather bountiful looking, if I do say! It's the perfect end to a summer day, and I imagine you sitting on the deck or balcony or at the picnic table, enjoying the twilight, a glass of something chilly, and this pretty salad. Even better, maybe you've harvested the beans, the tomatoes, or the potatoes (or all three!) from your garden. My grilled potatoes have been a hit with friends for years, so I had to include them in this composed salad, but with grilled shrimp, too, what's not to love? A pleasingly tangy vinaigrette ties this "fab four" together. I like to use square plates or big wide bowls for this salad. Then I arrange the four main ingredients in loose quadrants around the Bibb. To dress up the Bibb, add a little bit of mâche or a few sprigs of watercress. Be generous with the fresh herbs, too.

SERVES 4

1 ***To make the vinaigrette:*** In a glass measuring cup or glass jar with a tight-fitting lid, combine all the ingredients, including several grinds of fresh pepper—be generous! Whisk or shake vigorously until well combined. (If making ahead, be sure to bring to room temperature before using and mix again.)

2 ***To make the salad:*** Put the potatoes and 2 tsp salt in a Dutch oven or other large saucepan and add enough water to cover. Bring to a boil, reduce to a simmer, and cook until tender, 18 to 22 minutes. Drain, then spread the potatoes out on a few layers of dish towels and let sit for 15 to 20 minutes to steam off excess moisture.

3 ***Rinse the saucepan*** (or use a separate saucepan), fill it three-quarters full of water, and bring to a boil. Add the green beans and 1/2 tsp salt and cook until the beans are just tender, 4 to 6 minutes. Drain, arrange in a single layer on a dishcloth, and let cool.

12 oz/340 g small ripe **RED, ORANGE, YELLOW,** or other colorful **SMALL TOMATOES** (such as Green Zebra), cut into wedges

3 tbsp (any combination) **FRESH BASIL, MINT,** or **PARSLEY,** sliced, coarsely chopped, torn into small pieces, or left as whole small leaves

2 cups/40 g **MÂCHE** or **STEMMED WATERCRESS** (optional)

1 to 2 tbsp sliced **FRESH CHIVES, SCALLION GREENS,** and/or 8 to 12 small whole **EDIBLE FLOWERS** (such as chive blossoms or violets) for garnish (optional)

GRILLED BREAD (page 203) for serving (optional)

4 *Heat a gas grill to medium.* In a medium mixing bowl, combine the mayonnaise and mustard. Put the shrimp in another small bowl, season with 1/4 tsp salt, pepper, and 2 tsp of the mustard mixture, and toss until the shrimp are well coated. Halve the cooled potatoes and add them to the mustard mixture. Season with 1/2 tsp salt and toss gently until they are well coated.

5 *Arrange the shrimp in a single layer* on the grill, close the lid, and cook until well marked on the bottom, 2 to 3 minutes. Using tongs, turn and cook for 1 minute more. Transfer the shrimp to a bowl and cover loosely with aluminum foil. Put the potatoes, cut-side down, on the grill, lower the lid, and cook until well marked on the bottom, 3 to 5 minutes. (Don't disturb the potatoes for the first couple of minutes, or they will stick.) Using tongs, carefully turn the potatoes and cook them until the skin side is lightly browned, about 2 minutes more. Transfer the potatoes to a plate.

6 *Arrange four shallow bowls* or dinner plates on your counter. In a medium bowl, combine the tomatoes with half of the herbs and a pinch of salt. In a large bowl, combine the lettuce, mâche (if using), and the remaining herbs and sprinkle with a little salt. Put the green beans in a separate bowl. Whisk or shake the vinaigrette. Spoon 1 to 2 tbsp of the vinaigrette over the shrimp, 2 to 3 tbsp over the lettuces, 1 to 2 tbsp over the beans, and 2 tbsp over the tomatoes. Toss each gently, taste, and add a little more vinaigrette, if needed. Drizzle a little vinaigrette over the potatoes, as well.

7 *Mound the lettuce* on one side or in the center of each of the four dinner plates. Arrange one serving each of shrimp, potatoes, beans, and tomatoes up against the lettuce. Sprinkle each salad with a tiny bit of salt and drizzle each with a bit more vinaigrette, if necessary. (You will not use all the vinaigrette.) Garnish each serving with chives, scallions, and/or edible flowers (if using).

8 *Serve right away,* with the bread (if desired).

Grilled Sesame-Ginger Asparagus & Portobello Salad

with Napa-Spinach Slaw

¼ cup/60 ml **PEANUT OIL**, plus 2 tsp

2 tbsp **LOW-SODIUM SOY SAUCE**, plus 1 tsp

2 tbsp **RICE WINE**

1 tbsp **ASIAN SESAME OIL**

1 tbsp minced **GARLIC**

1 tbsp minced peeled **FRESH GINGER**

4 large **PORTOBELLO MUSHROOMS** (4 to 5 oz/115 to 140 g each), stemmed and gills scraped out with a spoon

¾ lb/340 g thin **ASPARAGUS** (32 to 36 thin spears, or 8 to 9 per salad), trimmed

KOSHER SALT

2 cups sliced **NAPA CABBAGE** (5 to 6 oz/140 to 170 g, use mostly leafy tops)

2 cups **BABY SPINACH LEAVES** (about 2½ oz/170 g)

¼ cup/20 g sliced **SCALLIONS** (white and light green parts)

2 tbsp chopped **FRESH CILANTRO**, plus 4 sprigs for garnish (optional)

2 tbsp freshly squeezed **LIME JUICE**

2 tsp **SUGAR**

1 to 2 tsp **TOASTED SESAME SEEDS**

{Summer Salads} On Martha's Vineyard, where I live, the birth of baby lambs in March and the appearance of the first asparagus tips poking through the soil in April are front-page news. Winters are long on the Island, and spring is highly anticipated. I think of this salad as a way to celebrate spring, and the deep shades of green in the asparagus, scallions, spinach, and cilantro make my heart sing. But the earthy grilled portobellos, boldly seasoned with ginger, garlic, and sesame, make this comforting, too. So I often brave the chilly air, turn on my grill, and make this before spring's official arrival. (Grill time is only 10 minutes). I'm never sorry, because this salad—and its sassy slaw—is bright and refreshing, and my friends love it, too. One tip: Dress the slaw right before serving. A few grilled sea scallops, a piece of grilled salmon, or even a bit of sushi rice could easily sneak onto the plate with this salad.

SERVES 4

1 ***In a glass liquid measure,*** combine the ¼ cup/60 ml peanut oil, 2 tbsp soy sauce, rice wine, sesame oil, garlic, and ginger. Whisk until well combined and transfer 3 tbsp of the mixture to a separate small bowl. Put the portobello caps, stem-side up, in a shallow 13-by-9-in/33-cm-by-23-cm baking dish and pour the remaining marinade into the four caps, drizzling a little around the top edges as well. Let sit for 30 minutes.

2 ***Stack the mushroom caps*** at one end of the baking dish and add the asparagus spears. Season the asparagus with ¼ tsp salt and roll the spears around in any of the marinade that has dripped off the mushrooms. (Tilt the mushroom caps and pour some of the residual marinade over the asparagus.) Add the remaining peanut oil to the pan to make sure the spears are well coated, and rub the bottom of the mushroom caps with some of the marinade-oil as well.

⟶

3 ***Heat a gas grill to medium-high.*** Put the portobello caps, stem-side up, on the grill, close the lid, and cook until they are very well browned or marked on the bottoms, 5 to 8 minutes. There should be a lot of liquid in the caps, and it should be simmering (which helps cook the stubborn insides of the mushroom). Using tongs, carefully turn the caps over (the liquid will spill out, so beware of flare-ups) and cook, covered, until the edges of the stemmed side are browned, 3 to 5 minutes more. Transfer the mushrooms to a cutting board and let them cool for 1 to 2 minutes. Cut them on the diagonal into thin slices, keeping the slices of each mushroom together.

4 ***Put the asparagus on the grill.*** (You can cook these along with the mushrooms if you like.) Lower the lid and cook until nicely marked on the bottom, 1 to 2 minutes. Using tongs, carefully turn over the asparagus, a few spears at a time (keeping them at an angle to the grate), close the lid, and cook until the other side is just marked, about 1 minute. (Do not overcook; they will still be bright green.) Transfer the asparagus to a tray or plate.

5 ***Arrange four rectangular or oval plates*** (white is nice) on your counter. In a large mixing bowl, combine the cabbage, spinach, half of the scallions, and half of the cilantro. Add the lime juice, sugar, and remaining 1 tsp soy sauce to the reserved marinade. Whisk until well combined. Spoon all but about 1½ tbsp of the dressing over the cabbage-spinach mixture and toss well to thoroughly coat.

6 ***Divide the slaw mixture*** evenly among the four plates to make a "bed" for the veggies. Arrange one-quarter of the asparagus spears across each bed of slaw (a diagonal angle looks pretty) and then arrange one sliced mushroom over each salad in a similar pattern, so that the asparagus spears and mushroom slices cover the bed of slaw in an appealing pattern. Drizzle the remaining dressing over the four salads, top with the remaining scallions and cilantro, and sprinkle with the toasted sesame seeds. Garnish each salad with a cilantro sprig (if using). Serve right away.

Warm Winter Salad of Roasted Root "Fries"

with Shallot & Sherry-Maple Vinaigrette

FOR THE VEGETABLES

1 lb/455 g SWEET POTATOES, unpeeled, pointy ends trimmed, and cut into 2- to 3-in-/5- to 7.5-cm-long and 3/8-in-/1-cm-wide sticks

1 lb/455 g YUKON GOLD POTATOES, unpeeled, cut into 2- to 3-in-/5- to 7.5-cm-long and 3/8-in-/1-cm-wide sticks

1 lb/455 g PARSNIPS, trimmed, peeled, and cut into 2- to 3-in-/5- to 7.5-cm-long and 3/8-in-/1-cm-wide sticks

1/3 cup/75 ml EXTRA-VIRGIN OLIVE OIL

KOSHER SALT

FOR THE WARM VINAIGRETTE

1/3 cup/75 ml EXTRA-VIRGIN OLIVE OIL

1 large SHALLOT (about 1½ oz/40 g), finely chopped (1/3 cup)

KOSHER SALT

2 tbsp SHERRY VINEGAR

1 tbsp pure MAPLE SYRUP

1 tsp DIJON MUSTARD

1 tsp coarsely chopped FRESH THYME LEAVES

FRESHLY GROUND PEPPER

{Winter Salads} Who doesn't like fries, and oh how virtuous you can feel eating them with salad! Not only is this warm winter salad delicious, but it also looks like an autumn colors extravaganza with the sweet potatoes, potatoes, and parsnips piled high on frisée, arugula, and radicchio. A tasty warm shallot vinaigrette brings everything together. The "fries," of course, are not deep-fried but oven-roasted. The low-moisture parsnips get very crisp, while the high-moisture sweet potatoes get very sweet, but not as crisp. The potatoes turn a lovely golden color and get crisp in places. So, in the end, the salad has a variety of textures.

If you want to prep the greens ahead, keep them in a stainless-steel bowl in the fridge, covered with a damp cloth. Make the vinaigrette ahead, if you like, too, and gently reheat it over medium-low heat in a skillet before using. This generous salad is a meal-in-one for veggie lovers, but a side order of grilled or roasted sausages wouldn't be amiss here, either.

SERVES 4

1 ***To cook the vegetables:*** Preheat the oven to 450°F/230°C/gas 8. Line two large rimmed heavy-duty baking sheets with parchment. In a large, wide mixing bowl, combine the sweet potato sticks, the potato sticks, and the parsnip sticks with the olive oil and 1½ tsp salt. Toss well, divide evenly between the prepared baking sheets, and spread in a single layer. Roast, rotating the baking sheets once from front to back and between upper and lower oven racks (and flipping the veggies with a spatula, if you like) after 20 minutes of cooking, until the "fries" are nicely browned and tender, about 35 minutes. Let cool for a couple of minutes on the baking sheets and then combine the potatoes, sweet potatoes, and parsnips in a mixing bowl.

FOR THE SALAD

5 cups BABY ARUGULA LEAVES (about 3½ oz/100 g)

1 small or ½ large head FRISÉE (about 4 oz/115 g) or yellow inner leaves of CHICORY, torn into bite-size pieces (about 4 cups)

1 small or ½ large head RADICCHIO (about 4 oz/115 g), cored and leaves cut into ½-in-/1.25-cm-wide strips (2 cups)

KOSHER SALT

¼ cup/30 g chopped toasted PECANS or WALNUTS (optional; see page 198)

2 ***To make the vinaigrette:*** In a small nonstick skillet, heat the olive oil over medium-low heat. Add the shallots and a good pinch of salt and cook, stirring occasionally, until the shallots are "toasted," 7 to 8 minutes. (Watch the shallots carefully; they will be simmering in the oil for 5 minutes or so before they begin to turn brown. After that, browning happens quickly, and you don't want to overcook them, or the oil will be bitter.) Remove the skillet from the heat and let cool for 5 minutes. Add the sherry vinegar, maple syrup, mustard, thyme, 1/4 tsp salt, and several grinds of pepper. Whisk until well blended. (Alternatively, pour and scrape the shallot oil into a heatproof liquid measure, add the other ingredients, and whisk until well blended. This is a slightly less awkward way to make the vinaigrette).

3 ***To make the salad:*** In a large, wide, heatproof mixing bowl, combine the arugula, frisée, and radicchio. Set out four dinner plates.

4 ***Season the greens*** with a sprinkling of salt, drizzle them with 4 to 5 tbsp/60 to 75 ml of the warm vinaigrette, and toss well. Taste and add just a bit more vinaigrette, if necessary. Mound a quarter of the greens on each of the plates. Top each plate of greens with an equal amount (about 1 tbsp) of nuts (if using).

5 ***Season the roasted "fries"*** generously with more salt, dress them very lightly by drizzling them with just 1 to 2 tbsp of the warm vinaigrette, and toss well. Mound the "fries" high in the center of the greens. Serve right away, passing the remaining vinaigrette (if desired).

Roasted Beet & Shallot Salad

with Mint & Sopressata Crisps

FOR THE BEETS AND SHALLOTS
3 tbsp EXTRA-VIRGIN OLIVE OIL, plus 2 tsp

1¼ lb/570 g small or medium BEETS, scrubbed and trimmed but not peeled

KOSHER SALT

7 or 8 small SHALLOTS (about 6 oz/170 g), peeled and halved

FOR THE SALAD
6 oz/170 g inner leaves of ESCAROLE or a combination of half ESCAROLE and half FRISÉE, torn or chopped into bite-size pieces (about 6½ cups)

¼ medium RADICCHIO (about 2 oz/55 g), cut into ¾-in-/2-cm-wide strips

¼ cup/7 g thinly sliced FRESH MINT LEAVES

1 tbsp plus 1 tsp SHERRY VINEGAR

1 tbsp plus 1 tsp PURE MAPLE SYRUP

1 tsp DIJON MUSTARD

2 tsp EXTRA-VIRGIN OLIVE OIL, plus 3 tbsp

4 to 5 slices (1½ oz/40 g) very thinly sliced SOPRESSATA (I like Applegate Farms), cut into thin strips about ¼ in/6 mm wide

{Winter Salads} I can honestly say that beets weren't really my thing until I started roasting them. As with so many other vegetables, the high heat of the oven transforms the flavor of beets from something rather coy to something much more interesting, more caramelized. Ta-da! Now they're a delicious ingredient for warm salads. I love roasting them with shallots to use in a pretty salad of winter greens and creamy blue cheese. I add crunch with toasted walnuts and a fun garnish of crisp sopressata (cured salami). (For a still-delicious vegetarian salad, you can skip the sopressata crisps.) Roasting the beets takes about 1 hour and 20 minutes, but since the rest of the salad comes together easily, you can plan to do other things while the beets are cooking. Wait to make the warm dressing until serving time. You could also cook the beets ahead and reheat them in the microwave, or make the salad with room-temperature beets in warmer weather. For a hearty all-veggie meal, follow with a satisfying grain dish like Shorty's Brown Rice with Stir-Fried Carrots, Ginger, Mint & Toasted Almonds (page 149). Grilled or roasted lamb would be nice with this, too.

SERVES 4

1 ***To roast the beets and shallots:*** Preheat the oven to 450°F/230°C/gas 8. Line a heavy ceramic or heatproof glass 13-by-9-in/33-by-23-cm baking dish with one long (18 to 24 in/46 to 62 cm) piece of aluminum foil going lengthwise; then crisscross that piece with another long piece of foil going widthwise. Brush the top layer of foil with 1 tbsp of the olive oil.

2 ***Halve the beets*** through the stem and put the halves, cut-side down, on the cutting board. (To prevent staining, line the cutting board with parchment or brown paper, if you like.) Cut the halves into ¾-in-/2-cm-thick wedges. In a medium bowl, toss the beets with 2 tbsp of the olive oil and ¾ tsp salt. Transfer the beets to the foil-lined pan and arrange them in a single layer. In a small bowl, toss the shallots with the remaining 2 tsp olive oil and a big pinch of salt and sprinkle them over the beets. (They can brown a bit too much on the bottom of the pan.) Fold in the ends of the foil and crimp them to form a flat and relatively airtight package.

1 tsp minced **GARLIC**

KOSHER SALT

¾ cup/85 g **MAYTAG** or other **SWEET, CREAMY BLUE CHEESE**, crumbled while still cold

⅓ cup/35 g chopped **TOASTED WALNUTS** (see page 198)

CRUSTY BREAD, CROSTINI (page 201), or **GRILLED BREAD** (page 203) for serving (optional)

3 ***Roast, without removing the foil,*** for 1 hour and 20 minutes. Remove the baking dish from the oven, carefully peel back the foil (be wary of the steam—use a knife to open the foil), and check to see if the beets are tender. (A paring knife should glide through easily.) If not, use tongs to flip some of the beets over (they will be caramelized on the bottom), reseal the foil, and return the beets to the oven for 10 minutes more. Let the beets and shallots cool in the pan for a few minutes before transferring them to a mixing bowl. (The shallots will be very soft.)

4 ***To make the salad:*** Arrange four dinner plates on your counter. In a large mixing bowl, combine the escarole, radicchio, and half of the mint and toss. Set aside. In a small bowl, whisk together the vinegar, maple syrup, and mustard.

5 ***Heat the 2 tsp olive oil*** in a medium heavy nonstick skillet over medium heat. Add the sopressata strips and cook until they are crisp, 5 to 7 minutes. (They will turn a deep redbrick color, shrink, and puff up slightly above the oil.) Using a slotted spoon, transfer the sopressata to a paper towel–lined plate.

6 ***In a small skillet (preferably nonstick),*** heat the remaining 3 tbsp olive oil and the garlic over medium-low heat. When the oil is hot and the garlic begins to simmer, cook for just about 30 seconds more to infuse the oil (do not brown the garlic). Add the vinegar mixture and a big pinch of salt to the pan and whisk immediately as the mixture bubbles up. (A flat whisk works great here). Reduce the heat to low and continue whisking for 1 minute to bring the vinaigrette together somewhat. (It won't be completely blended.) Remove the pan from the heat.

7 ***Spoon 3 to 4 tbsp of the warm dressing*** over the greens and sprinkle them with a little salt. Toss well, taste, and add a little more dressing, if needed. Pour the remaining dressing (scraping out all the garlic from the pan) over the beets and shallots and toss well. Using tongs, arrange the beets and shallots around the greens, dividing them evenly among the four plates. If there is extra vinaigrette combined with beet juices, you can drizzle that over the salads, too.

8 ***Divide the blue cheese evenly*** among the salads, tucking it in among the beets and greens. Sprinkle the salads with the remaining mint, the walnuts, and the sopressata crisps. Serve right away, with bread (if desired).

Crispy Red Potato Patties

with Warm Asian Slaw & Limey Sauce

FOR THE POTATOES
16 BABY RED POTATOES of uniform size (about 1½ oz/40 g each)

KOSHER SALT

½ cup/120 ml CANOLA OIL

FOR THE LIMEY SAUCE
⅓ cup/75 ml MAYONNAISE

1 tbsp freshly squeezed LIME JUICE

½ tsp finely grated LIME ZEST

½ tsp finely minced GARLIC

KOSHER SALT

{Winter Salads} The crispy "smashed" potatoes in this recipe are one of my all-time favorite dishes. I've served them as a side, but I love to let them star in a warm salad, too. Here they provide the crispy, meaty, salty contrast to a lighter, brighter, Asian-inspired slaw of cabbage and spinach that's dressed with a lime-ginger-balsamic vinaigrette. The potatoes also get a drizzle of limey mayo—a super-easy sauce I first invented for sweet-potato fries. A bite of the crunchy potatoes, the tangy slaw, and the creamy sauce all together tastes pretty darn swell. The potatoes are fun to make: Boil them whole first, then crush with your palm while they're still warm. (Do this up to a day ahead.) Next, coat them with oil and roast until very crispy and golden. They wind up crunchy outside and tender inside—so good. This composed salad is a fun one for guests, so why not serve it as a second course after a bowl of Southwestern Spiced Butternut Squash & Apple Soup with Lime, Yogurt & Cilantro (page 34).

SERVES 4

1 ***To cook the potatoes:*** Preheat the oven to 475°F/240°C/gas 9. Line a heavy-duty rimmed baking sheet with aluminum foil and top with a piece of parchment. Put a double layer of dish towels on a large cutting board or your counter. Arrange the potatoes (preferably in a single layer) in a large Dutch oven and add enough water to cover them by at least 1½ in/4 cm. Add 2 tsp salt, cover loosely, and bring to a boil. Reduce to a simmer and cook, uncovered, until the potatoes are tender all the way through but not falling apart (check with a paring knife), 18 to 20 minutes.

2 ***Using tongs or a slotted spoon,*** transfer each potato to the dish towels, not touching, and let cool for a few minutes. Using another folded dish towel, gently press down on each potato to flatten it into a patty about ½ in/12 mm thick (or up to ¾ in/2 cm). The patties don't have to be perfectly even, and a few pieces of potato may break off. (No matter; you can still roast them.) Let the patties cool for a few minutes more, transfer them to the baking sheet, and let them cool for 10 to 15 minutes longer. (Or, at this point, you can hold the potatoes in the fridge, covered with plastic wrap, for up to 24 hours. Bring to room temperature before roasting.)

FOR THE ASIAN SLAW

1½ cups/100 g very thinly sliced NAPA or SAVOY CABBAGE (pale inner leaves only)

1 cup/85 g very thinly sliced RED CABBAGE

1 cup/30 g (packed) BABY SPINACH LEAVES

KOSHER SALT

1 tbsp BALSAMIC VINEGAR

1½ tsp freshly squeezed LIME JUICE

1½ tsp BROWN SUGAR

1 tbsp CANOLA OIL, plus 2 tsp

½ medium RED ONION, thinly sliced

1 tsp minced peeled FRESH GINGER

½ tsp minced GARLIC

2 tbsp thinly sliced SCALLIONS (white and green parts)

3 ***Sprinkle the potatoes*** with 1/4 tsp salt and pour the canola oil over them. Carefully flip the potatoes over and season again with a scant 1/2 tsp salt. Rub with some of the oil, making sure that the potatoes are well coated on all sides. Roast, carefully turning once with a spatula halfway through cooking, until they turn a deep orange brown (a little darker and crisper around the edges), 28 to 30 minutes.

4 ***To make the limey sauce:*** In a small bowl, combine the mayonnaise, lime juice, lime zest, garlic, and a pinch of salt. Whisk until well combined. Let sit for a few minutes to let the flavors blend. Refrigerate if making ahead.

5 ***To make the slaw:*** In a large heatproof mixing bowl, combine the napa cabbage, red cabbage, and spinach. Sprinkle the greens with 1/4 tsp salt. In a small bowl, combine the vinegar, lime juice, and brown sugar. In a medium heavy nonstick skillet, heat the 2 tsp canola oil over medium-high heat. Add the red onion and a pinch of salt and cook, stirring, until the onion is wilted and just starting to brown around the edges, 3 to 4 minutes. Transfer the onion to the bowl of greens and let the skillet cool for a few seconds off the heat.

6 ***Reduce the heat to medium-low,*** return the pan to the heat, and add the remaining 1 tbsp canola oil. When the oil is hot, add the ginger and garlic and cook, stirring, until very fragrant, about 1 minute. Add the vinegar mixture to the pan (scrape out all the brown sugar with a small spatula), stir vigorously to warm it through, and immediately remove the pan from the heat. Stir and scrape the hot dressing over the greens, tossing the greens with tongs as you pour. Toss thoroughly to coat well and to soften and wilt the greens just a bit. (The cabbage will still be crunchy.) Taste and add more salt (if desired).

7 ***Arrange four dinner plates*** on your counter. On one side of each plate arrange four potato patties, slightly overlapping. On the other side of each plate, mound a quarter of the slaw. Spoon some of the limey sauce over the potatoes (down the middle of the row of potatoes), and top each serving with the scallions. Serve right away.

CHAPTER 2

HEARTY SOUPS

Making a Hearty Soup: How It Works

I once had a job cooking in a busy gourmet market where I made a different soup every morning for three years. Okay, I didn't really make nine hundred different soups, but I did have to get creative—without going too crazy. Because a simple bowl of soup is really a complex cup of expectations, memories, and comfort. One day, for example, I made peanut soup, which I'd eaten (and loved) as a child in Colonial Williamsburg. But here in New England, the unfamiliar peanut soup sat in the warmer, bereft and ignored all day, while the clam chowder flew out the door.

I learned a lot about myself as a cook and a lot about the world of eaters at that job. If you want to become a better cook, learn to make a good soup. If you want to make people happy, make them a bowl of soup (or chili!). And if you want something good to eat for yourself—something that happens to be a killer showcase for fresh vegetables, too—sit down to a bowl of Southwestern Spiced Butternut Squash & Apple Soup with Lime, Yogurt & Cilantro or Tuscan Kale & White Bean Soup with Rustic Croutons.

Every morning on that job, my first decision was creamy or chunky? Creamy (or puréed) soups are elegant and a great destination for veggies, so I usually made at least one for the weekend entertaining crowd. But chunky soups, with their casual personality, were popular all the time. So I've given you a choice in this chapter. The "creamy" soups (with not much cream!) each feature a different veggie: asparagus, mushrooms, squash, and tomatoes. Chunky soups, like Chilmark Harvest Chowder and Fall Farmers' Market Minestrone, are chock-full of different veggies. Lastly—in its own special category—is my delicious Smoky Chipotle Black Bean Chili with Roasted Vegetables, Fresh Salsa & Rice Pilaf.

Amazingly, all the soups rely on the same flavor principles; learn these and you're well on your way to becoming a good soup maker:

1 A soup is built on layers of flavor: Start from the bottom up with pungent aromatics (think onions, leeks, shallots, garlic, ginger) and fresh spices, brown veggies for deeper flavor, add interesting liquids, and finish with fresh herbs and a crunchy contrast of nuts or croutons.

2 Season as you go, starting at the very beginning, but never be afraid to season at the end, too. Nothing picks up the flavor of a soup like a squeeze of lemon or a splash of vinegar once it comes off the stove. (Along the way, add salt in small amounts.)

A few bonus tips for veggie soups: (A) Avoid packaged veggie broths. They vary widely in quality and can be too strongly seasoned (celery salt anyone?). I don't call for them in these soups. (B) Use a standing blender (not an immersion blender) for the creamy soups, and be sure to follow the precautions in the recipes. (C) Don't be afraid to stray from your comfort zone. The Spicy Noodle Hot Pot Soup with Bok Choy, Shiitake Mushrooms, Ginger, Lime & Peanuts sounds exotic, but it's quick, satisfying, and was one of my testers' favorites.

Creamy Double-Mushroom Soup

½ oz/15 g dried PORCINI MUSHROOMS

3 tbsp UNSALTED BUTTER, plus 1 tsp

2 tbsp plus 1 tsp EXTRA-VIRGIN OLIVE OIL

2 lb/910 g CREMINI or BABY BELLA MUSHROOMS (not stemmed), 4 small mushrooms reserved for garnish and the remainder cut into thick slices

KOSHER SALT

2 tsp minced GARLIC

2 tsp chopped FRESH ROSEMARY, plus an extra pinch

FRESHLY GROUND PEPPER

⅓ cup/75 ml DRY SHERRY

½ tsp SHERRY VINEGAR

¼ cup/60 ml HEAVY CREAM

FRESH PARSLEY or CHIVE leaves (optional)

CROSTINI (page 201) for serving (optional)

{Creamy Soups} Packed with mushroom flavor, this creamy soup gets its personality from both dried porcini mushrooms and lots of fresh cremini mushrooms. Dried mushrooms are naturally intense in flavor, and rehydrating them gives you a bonus soup ingredient: mushroom water. You can find dried porcini in most grocery stores. While cremini mushrooms (or baby bellas) are more flavorful than white mushrooms, I still like to give them an extra flavor boost by browning them. This easy-to-make soup comes together when the cremini and porcini simmer briefly with a bit of rosemary and garlic. The only tricky part is the blending: For the least splashing (and a smooth texture), put equal amounts of liquid and mushrooms into the blender jar with each batch you purée. Remember to fill the blender jar no more than about halfway, too. A simple garnish of a few sautéed cremini makes a pretty finish.

SERVES 4

1 ***In a medium saucepan,*** bring 2 cups/480 ml of water to a boil. Add the porcini mushrooms, remove the pan from the heat, and let soak for 30 minutes. Line a mesh strainer with a double layer of cheesecloth and put it over a bowl. Strain the porcini, squeezing the porcini in the cheesecloth to wring out as much liquid as possible; reserve the liquid. Discard the cheesecloth and finely chop the porcini. Measure the liquid in the bowl and add as much water as necessary to make 2 cups/480 ml. Add 4 cups/960 ml water for a total of 6 cups/1.4 L liquid.

2 ***In a large Dutch oven*** or other wide 6-qt/5.7-L soup pot, heat the 3 tbsp butter and 1 tbsp of the olive oil over medium heat. Add the thickly sliced cremini mushrooms and 1 tsp salt. Stir well, cover, and cook, stirring occasionally, until the cremini have released some liquid and the liquid is simmering, 6 to 8 minutes. Uncover, raise the heat to medium-high, and continue to cook (more liquid will be released), stirring occasionally, until all the liquid has evaporated and the pan is dry, 12 to 15 minutes. Add 1 tbsp of the olive oil to the mushrooms and continue cooking, stirring frequently, until most of the mushrooms have darkened and shrunk and many of them are turning an orangey brown on one side, another 7 to 9 minutes. (Don't allow the bottom of the pan to blacken.)

3 ***Add the garlic,*** 2 tsp rosemary, 1/2 tsp salt, and several grinds of pepper and stir until fragrant, about 30 seconds. Add the dry sherry and cook until it is almost completely reduced (this will happen quickly). Add the finely chopped porcini and the mushroom-soaking liquid, and bring to a boil. Reduce to a simmer and cook, uncovered, for 5 minutes. Remove the pan from the heat and let the soup cool for 15 minutes.

4 ***Meanwhile, cut the reserved cremini mushrooms*** into thin slices. In a small (8-in/20-cm) nonstick skillet, heat the remaining 1 tsp butter with the remaining 1 tsp olive oil over medium heat. Add the sliced mushrooms, a pinch of salt, and the pinch of rosemary and cook, turning with tongs when necessary, until the slices are nicely browned on both sides (they will have shrunk), 4 to 5 minutes.

5 ***In a blender, purée the soup*** in three batches, filling the jar only about halfway and taking care to distribute the solids and liquids evenly. Partially cover the lid with a folded dish towel (leaving a vent uncovered to let out steam) to prevent hot soup from splashing you. In a large mixing bowl, combine the three batches and then return the soup to the (rinsed) pot. Add the sherry vinegar and cream and whisk until well blended. Taste the soup and season with more salt and pepper (if desired). (It's best to taste the soup for seasoning when it's hot, as the flavors will be more pronouced. So if you're serving it right away, go ahead and reheat it gently on the stove before doing the final seasoning. If you're not serving right away, microwave a small portion for just a few seconds to test the seasoning.)

6 ***Divide the soup*** evenly among four shallow bowls. Garnish each with a few sautéed cremini slices and a fresh parsley or chive leaf or two for color (if using) and serve with crostini on the side (if desired).

Southwestern Spiced Butternut Squash & Apple Soup

with Lime, Yogurt & Cilantro

1 tsp GROUND CORIANDER

1 tsp GROUND CUMIN

½ tsp GROUND ANCHO CHILE

½ tsp UNSWEETENED COCOA

½ tsp SUGAR

¼ tsp GROUND CINNAMON

KOSHER SALT

¼ cup/60 ml APPLE CIDER

1 tsp LOW-SODIUM SOY SAUCE

2 tbsp EXTRA-VIRGIN OLIVE OIL

2 tbsp UNSALTED BUTTER

2 cups medium-diced ONION from about 2 medium onions

1½ lb/680 g peeled BUTTERNUT SQUASH from about 1 medium squash, cut into medium (¾-in/2-cm) pieces

2 tsp minced GARLIC

1 GOLDEN DELICIOUS APPLE (about 7 oz/200 g), peeled, cored, and cut into ¾-in/2-cm pieces (about 1½ cups)

2 tbsp chopped FRESH CILANTRO

¼ cup/70 g FULL-FAT GREEK YOGURT

½ tsp finely grated LIME ZEST

½ to 1 tsp freshly squeezed LIME JUICE

2 to 3 tbsp finely chopped TOASTED PECANS for garnish (optional; see page 198)

{Creamy Soups} I love butternut squash soup, but I'm often disappointed when I order it in restaurants. It can be bland and boring, and that's a shame, because butternut is the perfect canvas for painting a really flavorful soup. Plus, when cooked properly, it lends a lovely velvety texture to a puréed soup. For this soup, I've combined the butternut with a little apple for an especially nice texture (and a touch of sweetness), and I've given the soup a Southwestern spin with a passel of spices that includes cumin, coriander, ground ancho chile, cinnamon, and even cocoa. It smells amazing when it's cooking, but don't panic when you see how brown it is. Once you purée it, it becomes the most lovely shade of ochre, the spices fade into perfect balance with the other ingredients, and the finish of lime, yogurt, and cilantro make it all work together in harmony. Harmonious, yes, but definitely not boring.

SERVES 4

1 ***In a small bowl,*** combine the coriander, cumin, ground ancho chile, cocoa, sugar, cinnamon, and 1 tsp salt. Set aside. In a small liquid measure, combine the apple cider and soy sauce. Set aside.

2 ***In a large Dutch oven,*** heat the olive oil and butter over medium heat. When the butter has melted, add the onions and 1/2 tsp salt and stir well. Cover and cook, stirring occasionally, until the onions are softened and beginning to turn brown, about 8 minutes. Add the butternut squash and 1/4 tsp salt. Cover and cook until the squash is softened (it won't be completely tender) and has taken on some browning and the onions are lightly browned (the bottom of the pan will be brown), stirring occasionally at first, as the squash steams, and more frequently, scraping the bottom of the pan, as it begins to brown, 12 to 14 minutes more.

3 ***Uncover the pot,*** add the garlic, and cook, stirring, until softened and fragrant, about 30 seconds. Add the spice mixture and stir well. Add the cider–soy sauce mixture and stir well, scraping any browned bits off the bottom of the pot. Add the apple and 5 cups/1.2 L water, stir, and bring to a boil. Reduce to a gentle simmer and cook, uncovered, stirring and scraping the sides occasionally, for 15 minutes to blend the flavors and to finish cooking the squash and apple. Let the soup cool for 10 to 15 minutes.

4 ***In a blender, purée the soup*** in three batches, filling the jar only about halfway or just a little more and partially covering the lid with a folded dish towel (leaving a vent uncovered to let out steam) to prevent hot soup from splashing you. In a large mixing bowl, combine the three batches. Whisk in the yogurt, cilantro, lime zest, and 1/2 tsp of the lime juice. Taste the soup for seasoning and add more salt, if needed. Return the soup to the (rinsed) pot and gently reheat. Taste again and season with more salt or more lime juice (if desired).

5 ***Serve hot,*** garnished with the toasted pecans (if using).

Zesty Tomato-Ginger Bisque

2 tbsp ORANGE JUICE

1 tbsp HONEY

1 tbsp TOMATO PASTE or SUN-DRIED TOMATO PASTE

½ tsp BALSAMIC VINEGAR

Two 28-oz/795-g CANS WHOLE, PEELED TOMATOES (I like Muir Glen.)

2 tbsp EXTRA-VIRGIN OLIVE OIL

2 tbsp UNSALTED BUTTER

3 medium or 4 small LEEKS, white and pale green parts only, thoroughly washed and cut crosswise into thin slices (1½ cups, about 5½ oz/155 g)

1 small FENNEL BULB stemmed, quartered, cored, and thinly sliced (1½ cups)

KOSHER SALT

½ tsp GROUND CORIANDER

2 tbsp minced peeled FRESH GINGER

2 tsp minced GARLIC

½ cup/120 ml HALF-AND-HALF

FRESHLY GROUND PEPPER

24 to 28 RUSTIC CROUTONS (page 199)

{Creamy Soups} I have made tomato soups every which way, and I have to tell you, they're all pretty comforting. But this one has a special zing and warmth to it that I love, thanks to a layering of flavors. I start with leeks and fennel, add lots of ginger and a bit of garlic, and then season with a combination of orange, coriander, honey, and balsamic vinegar (just a small amount) to give those bright tomatoes a sturdy backbone. The magic of the blender produces a smooth, comforting purée, and a smattering of crunchy Rustic Croutons provides a nice textural contrast. (You could dollop a little crème fraîche or yogurt on this soup, too.) A cup of this makes a perfect winter supper with a slice of the Broccoli and Cheddar Frittata with Red Potatoes & Scallions (page 86).

SERVES 4

1 *In a small bowl,* combine the orange juice, honey, tomato paste, and balsamic vinegar. Set aside.

2 *Empty the contents of both tomato cans* into a mixing bowl. Gently break up the tomatoes into smaller pieces with your hands (effective but messy!) or a pair of scissors. Add 1 cup/240 ml water to the tomatoes and set aside.

3 *In a large Dutch oven* or other wide saucepan, heat the olive oil and butter over medium-low heat. Add the leeks, fennel, and 1 tsp salt. Cover and cook, stirring occasionally, until softened, 8 to 10 minutes. Uncover, raise the heat to medium, and continue cooking, stirring frequently and scraping any browned bits off the bottom of the pan, until the vegetables are all browned in spots and the bottom of the pan is browning a lot, another 8 to 10 minutes.

4 ***Add the coriander and stir well.*** Add the ginger and garlic, and cook, stirring, until softened and fragrant, about 30 seconds. Add the orange juice–tomato paste mixture and the tomatoes and stir well to incorporate. Bring the soup to a boil and immediately reduce to a gentle simmer. Cook, uncovered, stirring occasionally, for 17 to 18 minutes. (You will notice that the soup has reduced a bit.) Remove the pan from the heat and let the soup cool for 15 to 20 minutes.

5 ***In a blender, purée the soup*** in three batches, filling the jar only about halfway or just a little more and partially covering the lid with a folded dish towel (leaving a vent uncovered to let out steam) to prevent hot soup from splashing you. In a large mixing bowl, combine the three batches and then return the soup to the (rinsed) pot. Whisk in the half-and-half. Taste the soup for seasoning and add more salt or pepper, if needed.

6 ***Reheat the soup very gently.*** Serve hot, garnished with the croutons.

Asparagus & Leek Bisque

with Crème Fraîche & Tarragon

2 tbsp UNSALTED BUTTER

1 tbsp EXTRA-VIRGIN OLIVE OIL

1½ cups thinly sliced LEEKS from about 3 large leeks, white and pale green parts only (about 5½ oz/155 g)

½ cup/55 g thinly sliced CELERY

KOSHER SALT

2 tsp minced peeled FRESH GINGER

¼ cup/60 ml DRY WHITE WINE (such as Sauvignon Blanc)

1½ lb/680 g trimmed ASPARAGUS from about 3 bunches of medium-thin asparagus spears, cut into ½-in-/12-mm-long pieces), plus 3 trimmed spears, cut on the diagonal into 1-in-/2.5-cm-long pieces for garnish

¼ cup/55 g CRÈME FRAÎCHE

1½ to 2 tsp chopped FRESH TARRAGON

½ tsp finely grated LEMON ZEST

10 to 12 CROSTINI (page 201), spread with a bit of WARM GOAT CHEESE and a few thin slivers of SMOKED SALMON (optional)

{Creamy Soups} This is a lovely, satisfying soup with the light flavors of spring but the hearty backup of earthy sautéed leeks. I love how well the crème fraîche, tarragon, and lemon work with the asparagus at the end, making this one of my very favorite "creamy" soups. When you're shopping for asparagus, go ahead and buy four bunches of medium-thin stalks (bunches are usually about 1 lb/455 g each) to be safe (unless you find much bigger bunches!). You'll be trimming the tough ends to wind up with 1½ lb/680 g for the soup, plus you'll be cutting up a few stalks to blanch and use for garnish. This soup calls for a few Crostini on the side, topped with warm goat cheese, perhaps, and maybe a little smoked salmon. You could also follow it with a slice of any of the frittatas (on pages 82 to 88), or serve it simply on its own.

SERVES 4

1 ***In a large Dutch oven*** or other large sauce pot, heat the butter and olive oil over medium heat. Add the leeks, celery, and 1/2 tsp salt. Stir, cover, and cook, stirring once or twice, until the vegetables are mostly softened, about 5 minutes. Uncover and continue to cook, stirring frequently, until the vegetables have shrunk and the leeks have taken on some golden color, 7 to 8 minutes more.

2 ***Add the ginger and stir until fragrant,*** about 30 seconds. Add the white wine and cook until mostly reduced (this will happen quickly). Add the 1½ lb/680 g of sliced asparagus, 1 tsp salt, and 5½ cups/1.3 L water. Bring to a boil, reduce to a simmer, and cook, uncovered, until the asparagus are just tender, about 7 minutes. Remove the pan from the heat and let the soup cool for 15 minutes.

→

3 ***Meanwhile, bring a small saucepan of water to a boil*** with 1/4 tsp salt. Drop in the remaining asparagus pieces and cook until firm-tender but still bright green, 2 to 3 minutes. Drain and set aside for garnish.

4 ***In a blender, purée the soup*** in three batches, filling the jar only about halfway or just a little more and partially covering the lid with a folded dish towel (leaving a vent uncovered to let out steam) to prevent hot soup from splashing you. In a large mixing bowl, combine the three batches and then return the soup to the (rinsed) pot. Whisk in the crème fraîche, 1 1/2 tsp of the tarragon, and the lemon zest. Taste the soup for seasoning and add more salt or the remaining 1/2 tsp tarragon (if desired). (If you plan to eat the soup right away, you will most likely want to add the remaining 1/2 tsp tarragon. If you plan to eat it later, hold back, as the tarragon intensifies just slightly over time.)

5 ***Reheat the soup very gently.*** Serve hot, garnished with the reserved asparagus pieces and with the crostini on the side (if desired).

Tuscan Kale & White Bean Soup

with Rustic Croutons

3 tbsp EXTRA-VIRGIN OLIVE OIL

1 medium or 2 small ONIONS, cut into medium (¾-in/2-cm) dice (about 1⅓ cups)

1 medium CARROT, cut into ⅜-in dice (scant ½ cup)

2 oz/55 g very thinly sliced PANCETTA, diced (about ½ cup)

KOSHER SALT

1 tbsp finely chopped GARLIC

About 2 bunches TUSCAN KALE, stemmed and leaves torn into 1- to 2-in/2.5- to 5-cm pieces (6 to 7 cups/140 to 155 g)

FRESHLY GROUND PEPPER

3 cups/720 ml LOW-SODIUM CHICKEN BROTH

One 15½-oz/445-g can SMALL WHITE BEANS, drained

2 to 3 tsp freshly squeezed LEMON JUICE

¼ to ⅓ cup (about 1 to 1.5 oz/ 30 to 40 g coarsely grated PARMIGIANO-REGGIANO

RUSTIC CROUTONS (page 199)

{Chunky Soups} This soup is all about the greens, the beans, and the hunky croutons. It's a delicious variation on the classic Italian escarole and white bean soup, which has a scant amount of broth in comparison to the good "stuff" that fills the bowl. Here I've found the perfect place to highlight the beautiful and delicious dark green kale known as Tuscan kale (a.k.a. lacinato or cavolo nero). This is one soup where I do use a little meat (pancetta) and chicken broth for quick flavor. It's best eaten as soon as it's made. The canned beans I use most often for this soup are Goya brand "small white beans," but if you can't find them, use Great Northern or other small white beans. Cannellini beans are too large.

SERVES 4

1 ***In a large Dutch oven*** or other soup pot, heat the olive oil over medium heat. Add the onion, carrot, pancetta, and ¼ tsp salt. Cover the pot and cook, stirring occasionally, until the onion has softened, 5 to 6 minutes. Uncover and continue cooking, stirring frequently, until the veggies have shrunk and many are nicely browned (and leaving browned bits on the bottom of the pan), another 6 to 7 minutes. Add the garlic, stir, and cook until fragrant, about 30 seconds. Add the kale and season with ¾ tsp salt and a few grinds of pepper. Stir the kale with tongs as it begins to wilt, mixing it well with the contents of the pot. Stir in the broth and 2 cups/ 480 ml water and bring to a boil. Reduce to a simmer and cook, covered, until the kale is tender, 8 to 10 minutes. Add the beans and simmer, uncovered, 2 minutes more. Stir in 1 to 2 tsp of the lemon juice and remove the pan from the heat. Taste the soup and adjust the seasoning, adding more salt, pepper, or lemon juice, if desired.

2 ***Ladle the soup into four shallow soup bowls.*** Top each with a quarter of the Parmigiano and a quarter of the Rustic Croutons. Serve right away.

Spicy Noodle Hot Pot

with Bok Choy, Shiitake Mushrooms, Ginger, Lime & Peanuts

KOSHER SALT

6 oz/170 g FRESH CHINESE EGG NOODLES, torn into slightly shorter pieces

½ tsp ASIAN SESAME OIl

1 tbsp SOY SAUCE

1 tbsp freshly squeezed LIME JUICE

1 tsp packed BROWN SUGAR

2 tsp PEANUT or VEGETABLE OIL, plus 2 tbsp

One 3½-oz/100-g package FRESH SHIITAKE MUSHROOMS, stemmed and thinly sliced

3 small SHALLOTS (about 3 oz/85 g), thinly sliced

1 lb/455 g BOK CHOY (both leaves and stalks), cored, washed thoroughly, and then thinly sliced crosswise

1 tbsp chopped peeled FRESH GINGER

1 tbsp chopped GARLIC

½ tsp ASIAN CHILI-GARLIC SAUCE

2 cups/480 ml LOW-SODIUM CHICKEN BROTH

3 to 4 tbsp chopped FRESH CILANTRO

3 to 4 tbsp chopped ROASTED PEANUTS

2 tbsp finely sliced SCALLIONS

{Chunky Soups} For such a quick soup, this one is darn satisfying. Thanks to the bold flavors of ginger, lime, soy sauce, and cilantro—and the intriguing flavor of one of my favorite greens, bok choy—the soup packs a punch without much fuss. I do take one extra little step and sauté the shiitake mushrooms separately in a nonstick pan; otherwise they can stick before browning or cooking through. I also take a cue from Asian cooks and boil the soup noodles separately. (They can soak up a lot of liquid if added raw to the soup.) This works out nicely, as it means you can distribute the noodles evenly among the soup bowls and then add the tasty broth, the greens, and the fun condiments. Heads of bok choy vary tremendously. You can use any size; just cut a bit off the bottom, quarter lengthwise, and slice crosswise. Use plenty of the leafy tops, where there's lots of flavor. If you can't find fresh Chinese egg noodles (in the produce section of the grocery), substitute with another fresh egg pasta such as Italian linguine.

SERVES 4

1 ***Bring a large pot of salted water to a boil.*** Add the egg noodles and cook until tender, 2 to 3 minutes. Drain in a colander, rinse briefly, and let dry a bit. Transfer to a bowl and toss with a big pinch of salt and the sesame oil.

2 ***In a small bowl,*** stir together the soy sauce, lime juice, and brown sugar. Set aside.

3 ***In a medium nonstick skillet,*** heat the 2 tsp peanut oil over medium-low heat. Add the shiitake mushrooms and a pinch of salt and cook, stirring, until tender and just starting to brown, 6 to 7 minutes. Remove from the heat and reserve.

4 ***In a large Dutch oven*** or other soup pot, heat the remaining 2 tbsp peanut oil over medium-low heat. Add the shallots and a pinch of salt, and cook, stirring, just until the shallots have softened and many are browning, 3 to 4 minutes. Add the bok choy and 1/2 tsp salt and stir until all the leaves have wilted, about 2 minutes. Add the ginger, garlic, and chili-garlic sauce and stir until fragrant, about 30 seconds. Add the cooked shiitake mushrooms, the chicken broth, and 2 cups/480 ml water to the pot. Bring to a boil, reduce to a simmer, and cook 5 minutes. Remove the pot from the heat and let sit for 5 minutes. Stir in the soy-lime mixture and 2 tbsp of the cilantro.

5 ***Divide the noodles*** evenly among four deep soup bowls. Using tongs, divide the greens evenly, placing them over the noodles, and then ladle equal amounts of the remaining broth and soup contents over each.

6 ***Garnish each bowl of soup*** with the remaining cilantro, peanuts, and scallions. Serve right away with both a fork and spoon.

Fall Farmers' Market Minestrone

¼ cup/60 ml EXTRA-VIRGIN OLIVE OIL

1 large or 2 medium ONIONS, cut into 3/4-in/2-cm pieces (about 2 cups/225 g)

½ small FENNEL BULB, quartered, cored, and thinly sliced (about 1 cup/100 g)

¼ small head SAVOY CABBAGE, thinly sliced (about 2 cups/130 g)

2 CARROTS, cut crosswise into thin slices (about 1 cup/115 g)

KOSHER SALT

1 tbsp minced GARLIC

1 tbsp chopped FRESH THYME

2 tsp chopped FRESH ROSEMARY

1 tsp GROUND CORIANDER

1 tbsp TOMATO PASTE

1 cup/125 g peeled, medium (¾-in/2-cm) diced BUTTERNUT SQUASH

1 cup/150 g large (1-in/2.5 cm) diced stemmed SWISS CHARD leaves (thinly slice stems separately and include them, too)

One 14½-oz/415-g can DICED TOMATOES (I like Muir Glen), well drained

One 2-in/5-cm piece PARMIGIANO-REGGIANO rind, plus ⅓ cup/40 g coarsely grated PARMIGIANO-REGGIANO

½ cup/70 g DRIED DITALINI PASTA (or other very small pasta)

{Chunky Soups} In late fall, the biggest farmers' market on the Island moves inside to the Agricultural Hall, which is right across the street from my house. Oh joy! On Saturdays, all we have to do is pull on our boots and trot over there. And because our autumns are mild, there are still lots of veggies around. (Even corn in early November.) So I created this soup in honor of the West Tisbury Farmers Market. Unlike many minestrones, this one is vegetarian, and my friends who tested this were amazed at the depth of flavor with no meat added. A lot of aromatic veggies and a nice richness from the Parmesan rind do the trick. I usually finish the soup with grated Parmigiano and/or a bit of gremolata (a mix of finely chopped fresh parsley, lemon zest, and garlic). But if you don't want to bother with the gremolata (after all that vegetable chopping!), the soup is delicious without it.

SERVES 6

1 *In a large Dutch oven* or other large soup pot, heat the olive oil over medium heat. Add the onion, fennel, cabbage, carrots, and 1 tsp salt. Cover and cook, stirring occasionally, until the onion has softened and is mostly translucent, and the cabbage is limp, 6 to 8 minutes. Uncover and continue cooking, stirring occasionally, until much of the cabbage as well as the bottom of the pan are browning, another 8 to 9 minutes.

2 *Add the 1 tbsp garlic,* thyme, rosemary, coriander, and tomato paste. Stir until fragrant, about 30 seconds. Add the squash, chard, diced tomatoes, and 1½ tsp salt and stir until well incorporated. Add the Parmigiano rind and 8 cups/2 L water.

1 cup/115 g thinly sliced GREEN BEANS

½ to 1 cup/85 to 155 g FRESH CORN KERNELS, cut from 1 medium cob (optional; see page 213)

1 to 2 tsp freshly squeezed LEMON JUICE

FRESHLY GROUND PEPPER

GREMOLATA
½ tsp minced GARLIC

½ tsp finely grated LEMON ZEST

2 tbsp chopped FRESH PARSLEY

3 ***Bring to a boil,*** reduce to a simmer, and cook, stirring occasionally, for 10 minutes. Add the pasta and cook for another 8 minutes. Add the green beans and corn (if using) and cook 4 to 5 minutes more. Remove the pot from the heat, remove the Parmigiano rind, and stir in 1 tsp of the lemon juice. Let cool for a few minutes and then taste and adjust the seasoning, adding salt, pepper, and the remaining lemon juice.

4 ***To make the gremolata:*** Combine the garlic, lemon zest, and parsley in a small bowl.

5 ***Garnish each portion of hot soup*** with some of the gremolata and some of the grated Parmigiano. Serve immediately.

Chilmark Harvest Chowder

3 medium ears fresh SWEET CORN, shucked

1 large GARLIC CLOVE, smashed, plus 1 tbsp minced

1 cup/240 ml HEAVY CREAM

3 BACON SLICES

2 tbsp UNSALTED BUTTER

3 small to medium LEEKS (white and light green parts only), thinly sliced and thoroughly washed (about 1½ cups/155 g)

2 large CELERY STALKS, thinly sliced (about 1 cup/115 g)

KOSHER SALT

¼ cup/60 ml DRY SHERRY

2 cups/480 ml CLAM JUICE (I like Snow's brand.)

½ lb/225 g YUKON GOLD POTATOES (unpeeled), cut into ½-in/12-mm dice

½ lb/225 g peeled BUTTERNUT SQUASH, cut into ½-in/12-mm dice

½ lb/225 g GREEN BEANS, trimmed and cut into ½-in/12-mm pieces

½ lb/225 g WHITE FISH FILLETS (such as Pacific cod or striped bass), cut into 1-in/2.5-cm pieces

½ lb/225 g SCALLOPS (preferably bay scallops)

{Chunky Soups} When I first got to the Vineyard, I often meandered up to the fishing village of Menemsha at the far end of the Island. The docks drew me like a magnet, and while I strolled along them, watching the fishermen at work, any negative energy I came with slipped away. Of course, I always bought fish, and I started inventing my own chowder (on this very chowdery of islands).

Fast-forward two summers, and I had my first big vegetable garden—way Up-Island, too, on a farm in the town of Chilmark (which includes Menemsha). So one day, I made my Menemsha Fish Chowder with less fish and lots of veggies. Voilà, Chilmark Harvest Chowder. Since then, I've tweaked this recipe a bit, but it still includes fish and a few of our iconic bay scallops. And a bit of bacon, too. No, this one isn't vegetarian, but it is a great destination for late-summer veggies. For the best texture, don't overcook the veggies. Just add them in order of cooking time, as the recipe instructs, and you'll be happy. For the best flavor, taste and season generously at the end, with both freshly ground pepper and a little of the lemon and thyme that I suggest.

SERVES 4 OR 5

2 tsp roughly chopped **FRESH THYME LEAVES**

1/2 to 1 tsp finely grated **LEMON ZEST**

FRESHLY GROUND PEPPER

1 *Snap each ear of corn in half.* Cut the kernels from each cob half and reserve the cobs. You should have about 1 3/4 cups/275 g kernels. In a 3-qt/2.8-L sauce pot, combine the smashed garlic, the corn kernels, and cream. Over the pot, scrape the "milk" and juice from each corncob by running the back of a paring knife down its length. Discard the cobs. Put the pot over medium-high heat and bring just to a boil (watch carefully so that it does not boil over). Immediately remove it from the heat and let the mixture steep, giving it a stir from time to time, until you are ready to add it to the soup, about 15 minutes.

2 *Meanwhile, in a large Dutch oven* or other large soup pot, cook the bacon over low to medium-low heat until crisp, about 12 minutes. Transfer the bacon to a paper towel–lined plate and let cool. Crumble the bacon and set aside. Raise the heat to medium. Add the butter, leeks, and celery to the pot; season with 1/2 tsp salt; and stir, scraping up any browned bits from the bottom of the pot. Cover and cook, stirring occasionally, until the leeks and celery have softened, 5 to 6 minutes. Uncover and continue cooking until the vegetables have shrunk and are lightly browned, another 4 to 6 minutes.

3 *Add the minced garlic* and stir until fragrant, about 1 minute. Add the sherry and simmer, stirring, until the liquid is mostly reduced, about 1 minute. Add the clam juice, potatoes, 1 cup water, and 1 tsp salt to the pot. Bring to a boil, reduce to a simmer, and cook, loosely covered (leaving the lid just slightly askew), for 5 minutes. Add the squash, return to a simmer, and cook, partially covered, for 5 minutes more. Add the green beans, return to a simmer, and cook, partially covered, for 5 minutes more.

4 *Meanwhile, add the fish* and scallops (if using sea scallops, quarter them; leave bay scallops whole) to the pot and cook at a very gentle simmer (barely bubbling), partially covered, until the fish and scallops are just cooked through, 4 to 5 minutes. Uncover, add the cream-corn mixture (including the garlic pieces), and stir well. Bring just to a simmer and remove the pot from the heat.

5 *Stir in 1 tsp of the thyme,* 1/2 tsp of the lemon zest, and several grinds of pepper. Let the soup cool and rest for a few minutes. (It will be easier to taste, and the flavors need a couple of minutes to start to meld.) Taste and adjust the seasoning by adding more pepper, salt, fresh thyme, and lemon zest (add zest just a little at a time), if needed.

6 *Serve right away,* garnished with the crumbled bacon.

Smoky Chipotle Black Bean Chili

with Roasted Vegetables, Fresh Salsa & Rice Pilaf

{Chili} Personally, I'm not so fond of "vegetable" chilis, as they seem to feature overcooked and watery veggies that were never meant to be "stewed." But a robustly flavored bean chili topped with roasted vegetables, now that's my thing. I've always taken this approach with pot roast or beef stew veggies: Instead of adding them to the pot during braising, I roast them separately and garnish the dish with them. So I've taken this idea and created a deeply flavorful bean chili (vegetarian, yes) that I use as a base for showcasing vegetables. In winter, I top the chili with roasted vegetables like butternut squash or sweet potatoes. In warmer weather, I top the bean chili with a cool, salsa-like mixture of raw veggies such as tomatoes, avocado, and corn.

I always serve the chili over rice to balance the intense flavor and thick texture. (By the way, I call the chili spicy, rather than hot, because although it is intensely flavorful, it is not hot in the way that will alienate half your friends and family. My testers and their families all loved this.) Despite a long ingredient list, the chili actually takes less time to prepare than most long-cooking meat chilis, and it yields enough for entertaining or a few nights of dinner. I've called on the excellent supply of spices we have available to us now, including ground ancho chile and ground chipotle, as well as canned chipotles in adobo, to create a deeply flavored chili that doesn't require soaking dried chiles or long cooking. (I use canned beans, too.) All the spices I call for are available in grocery stores now, but if you can't find something, search online. It's worth using the right combination of spices for the best flavor.

⟶

1 tbsp plus 1 tsp GROUND ANCHO CHILE

1 tbsp GROUND CORIANDER

1 tbsp GROUND CUMIN

1 tbsp MEXICAN OREGANO

1 tbsp SWEET PAPRIKA

1 tbsp BROWN SUGAR

1½ tsp UNSWEETENED COCOA

¼ tsp GROUND (DRIED) CHIPOTLE CHILE

¼ tsp GROUND CINNAMON

¼ tsp GROUND CLOVES

KOSHER SALT

¼ cup/60 ml DRY RED WINE

¼ cup/65 g TOMATO PASTE

¼ cup/15 g finely chopped FRESH CILANTRO stems and leaves, plus 2 tbsp chopped fresh cilantro leaves and extra sprigs for garnish

2 tsp finely chopped CANNED CHIPOTLE CHILE IN ADOBO (about 1 small chipotle with sauce still clinging to it), plus 2 tsp adobo sauce from the can

1½ cups/360 ml CRUSHED TOMATOES (I like Cento brand; do not use ones with added herbs.)

2 tbsp UNSALTED BUTTER

2 tbsp EXTRA-VIRGIN OLIVE OIL

1 large or 2 medium ONIONS, cut into ¾-in/2-cm dice (about 2¼ cups)

1 large or 2 small GREEN or RED BELL PEPPERS, cut into ¾-in/2-cm dice (about 1½ cups)

1 tbsp plus 2 tsp minced GARLIC

With the shopping done, you'll only need a couple of hours in the kitchen, so plan to have friends over when you're done. This chili is one of my favorite entertaining dishes, because guests can customize their own dinners. In addition to the rice, the bean chili, and the vegetable toppings, I put out sour cream, goat cheese or *queso fresco*, cilantro sprigs, and toasted *pepitas*. Sometimes I also offer a bit of braised, shredded beef or roast chicken for meat lovers to layer on. Everyone gets to have the chili as he or she likes it: more rice, fewer beans, more veggies—whatever works! It's all delicious.

I like the chili best the same day it's made, but you can refrigerate it for three days or freeze it (in portions) for 1 month. The chili will feed six easily, so I've called for a double batch of White Rice Pilaf and 2 lb/910 g of roasting veggies in order to serve six people the whole dish. But if you want to serve the chili for eight, you can easily do so with a just a little more rice and vegetables.

SERVES 6

1 ***In a small bowl, combine the ground ancho chile,*** coriander, cumin, oregano, paprika, brown sugar, cocoa, ground chipotle, cinnamon, cloves, and 1½ tsp salt. Set aside.

2 ***In a liquid measure, whisk together*** the red wine, tomato paste, finely chopped cilantro stems and leaves, the chopped chipotle, and the adobo. Set aside.

3 ***In another large liquid measure or bowl,*** combine the crushed tomatoes with 3 cups/720 ml water and stir well.

4 ***In a large Dutch oven,*** heat the butter and olive oil over medium heat. When the butter has melted, add the onion, bell pepper, and ½ tsp salt and stir. Cover and cook, stirring occasionally, until the vegetables have softened, 5 to 7 minutes. Uncover, raise the heat to medium-high, and continue cooking until the onion is lightly browned, another 7 to 8 minutes. Reduce the heat to medium-low, add the garlic and jalapeño, and cook, stirring, until softened and fragrant, about 1 minute.

5 ***Add the dried spice mixture*** and cook, stirring and scraping until well incorporated, 20 to 30 seconds. Add the tomato paste mixture and cook, stirring and scraping it against the sides of the pan, for 1 to 2 minutes.

1½ tsp minced **FRESH JALAPEÑO**, seeds and ribs removed

Three 15½-oz/445-g cans **BLACK BEANS**, drained and rinsed

WHITE RICE PILAF (page 208; cook a double recipe to serve 6) or your own cooked rice

ROASTED WINTER VEGETABLES FOR CHILI (page 54) or **SUMMER VEGETABLE SALSA FOR CHILI** (page 55)

6 oz/170 g crumbled **GOAT CHEESE**, ***QUESO FRESCO***, or **SOUR CREAM** (optional)

⅔ cup/75 g toasted ***PEPITAS*** (optional)

6 **LIME WEDGES** (optional)

6 ***Add the crushed tomato mixture*** and cook, stirring and scraping the bottom of the pan, until well combined. Bring the mixture to a gentle simmer and cook, loosely covered, stirring occasionally and continuing to scrape the bottom of the pan, for 20 minutes. Keep an eye on the heat and reduce it, if necessary, to maintain a gentle simmer.

7 ***Uncover the pot and add the drained beans.*** Raise the heat to medium-high and return the chili to a simmer and then reduce the heat to medium-low and maintain a gentle simmer. Stir thoroughly and cook, partially covered, for 10 minutes.

8 ***Remove the pan from the heat*** and stir in the 2 tbsp chopped cilantro. The chili will stay warm, covered, off the heat for a half hour.

9 ***To serve, spoon 1 cup/155 g rice*** into each of six deep bowls and ladle about 1 cup/225 g chili over the rice. Top each serving with a large handful of Roasted Winter Vegetables for Chili or a generous spoonful of Summer Vegetable Salsa for Chili. Garnish each serving with your choice of goat cheese, *queso fresco*, or sour cream and/or cilantro sprigs, toasted *pepitas*, and lime wedges (if desired). (Alternatively, cool the chili, uncovered, at room temperature, stirring frequently, for 30 minutes. Then divide into portions and refrigerate until completely cold. Transfer to the freezer, if you like, and store up to 1 month, or refrigerate, covered, up to 3 days.)

Roasted Winter Vegetables for Chili

2 lb/910 g peeled and seeded BUTTERNUT SQUASH (weighed after peeling), cut into ½-in/12-mm dice (about 7 cups), or an equivalent amount of one or a combination of the following: CARROTS, PARSNIPS, SWEET POTATOES (orange or white), RUTABAGAS, or TURNIPS (No need to peel sweet potatoes or turnips.)

5 tbsp/75 ml EXTRA-VIRGIN OLIVE OIL

1¼ tsp KOSHER SALT

{Chili} I like roasted butternut squash best with the chili, but sweet potatoes and other roots are great, too. (Or you could roast a combo or a few choices.) I cut the veggies into ½-in/12-mm dice so that they cook quickly and make an easy-to-serve-and-eat topping for the chili. This amount of raw veggies will provide enough topping for six servings, but you can roast less to serve fewer people. If you want to roast more, don't crowd the sheet pans, or the veggies will steam; instead, roast in batches. Then gently reheat before serving, either in the oven or in the microwave.

MAKES 3½ CUPS

Preheat the oven to 450°F/230°C/gas 8. Line two large, heavy-duty, rimmed baking sheets with parchment. In a large mixing bowl, toss the diced vegetables with the olive oil and salt until thoroughly coated. Divide the vegetables evenly between the prepared baking sheets and spread them in a single layer. Roast for 18 minutes. Using a flat spatula, flip some of the veggies over for more even browning. Rotate the baking sheets from front to back and between top and bottom racks and roast until all the veggies are tender and nicely browned in places, about 12 minutes more, for a total of about 30 minutes. Use right away.

Summer Vegetable Salsa for Chili

3 tbsp EXTRA-VIRGIN OLIVE OIL

2 tbsp ORANGE JUICE

1 tbsp freshly squeezed LIME JUICE

1 tsp HONEY

KOSHER SALT

10 to 12 oz/280 to 340 g small CHERRY TOMATOES or GRAPE TOMATOES, halved or quartered (You can replace half of the tomatoes with husked and diced fresh tomatillos, if you like.)

2 ripe AVOCADOS (about 10 oz/280 g each), cut into 3/8-in/1-cm dice

1 small to medium ZUCCHINI, quartered lengthwise and thinly sliced crosswise (about 1¼ cups/170 g)

½ cup/75 g raw FRESH CORN KERNELS, cut from about 1 cob (optional; see page 213)

1 small RADISH, quartered and thinly sliced (optional)

2 tbsp CHOPPED FRESH CILANTRO

{Chili} To make things easier around serving time, whisk up the dressing and cut the veggies about 45 minutes ahead. Leave them both at room temperature, covered (toss the avocado with a little dressing to keep it from discoloring), then combine everything about 15 minutes before serving. (Any longer, and the veggies will shed too much water; also, refrigerating tomatoes robs them of flavor.)

MAKES 5 CUPS

In a mixing bowl, whisk together the olive oil, orange juice, lime juice, honey, and 3/4 tsp salt. Add the tomatoes, avocados, zucchini, corn (if using), radish (if using), and cilantro. Stir well and use right away, or let sit at room temperature for up to 20 minutes. Do not refrigerate.

CHAPTER 3

VEGGIE PASTA SAUCES

Making a Veggie Pasta Sauce: How It Works

There's probably no better way to get kids, dads, lovers, picky-eater friends—oh, just about everybody—to eat more vegetables than tucking them (the veggies, not the friends) into a pasta. But a so-called veggie pasta can be a scary thing. Visions of flavorless steamed veggies rolling around uncomfortably on a tangle of noodles come to mind. Dear me, where is the synchronicity? Just because a pasta features vegetables doesn't mean it shouldn't have a sauce—and flavor boosters—to bring the veggies and noodles together in happy harmony. (The veggies themselves need to be treated right, too.)

At the same time, it's not like we want to make long-simmering sauces every time we make pasta. It'd be nice to keep our main-dish veggie pastas mostly vegetarian, too, so chicken broth isn't a great option. That being the case, where are the sauce and the flavor coming from, you ask?

First, let me say that there are dozens of ways to prepare good main-dish pastas, but to keep things simple, I'm featuring just three methods in this chapter. The stovetop pastas feature stir-fried (yes, stir-fried) veggies that pick up extra flavor from aromatics like leeks, garlic, and ginger and from a little Italian trick: infused oils. Sizzling chopped garlic and crushed red pepper in olive oil, and drizzling that over, say, spaghetti, is a great flavor start even before the veggies get caramelized. (If you don't have one of the great nonstick, bowl-shaped stir-fry pans I love so much, use a deep sauté pan rather than a wok.)

The saucy part comes from another Italian trick: using the (now-starchy) pasta cooking water to make a pan sauce. I use it in combination with other flavorful liquids like citrus juices and, yes, sometimes a touch of cream. When the liquids go into the pan with the browned veggies, they pick up extra flavor from them, too. I finish with Parmigiano to bring the sauce and pasta together.

Baked pastas—the second part of this chapter—are so comforting and crowd-pleasing that everyone should have a "house" recipe for a rainy night. At our house, we love my delicious Quick-Roasted Plum Tomato Pizza Sauce (page 167) with pasta. I'm psyched if I've got a batch in the freezer (or the 45 minutes and the tomatoes to make it), because it's the perfect amount for Classic Baked Pasta with Roasted Tomato Sauce for Two. If not—and if I need a bigger amount of sauce—I'll make a streamlined stovetop sauce from pantry ingredients, again enhancing it with pasta cooking water. I roast or sauté hearty veggies, grate cheese, chop herbs, and mix up my pasta to bake until brown and bubbly, about 25 minutes.

While I'm not a big fan of pasta salads, I do like a room-temp or "cool" pasta in the summertime. There's no better place to highlight fresh, raw veggies like snow peas, spinach, scallions, tomatoes, and corn. Not surprisingly, the other key to delicious "cool" pastas is an assertive sauce or vinaigrette that will taste full-flavored even at room temperature when mixed with pasta. So use your best veggies here, and keep the pasta and sauce in proportion.

Orecchiette

with Lemony Broccoflower & Toasted Garlic Bread Crumbs

3 tbsp freshly squeezed LEMON JUICE

½ tsp finely grated LEMON ZEST

2 tsp HONEY

2 tsp DIJON MUSTARD

KOSHER SALT

½ lb/225 g DRIED ORECCHIETTE (ear-shaped pasta)

4 tbsp/55 g UNSALTED BUTTER (2 tbsp cut into pieces and kept cold in fridge)

2 tbsp EXTRA-VIRGIN OLIVE OIL, plus more if needed

1 lb/455 g BROCCOFLOWER or GREEN CAULIFLOWER FLORETS (from about 2 small heads or 1½ bigger heads), each cut about 1½ in/4 cm long and ½ to ¾ in/12 mm to 2 cm wide

1 small ONION (4 to 5 oz/115 to 140 g), cut into ¼-in/6 mm-thick slices

1 tbsp minced GARLIC

FRESHLY GROUND PEPPER

2 tbsp chopped FRESH PARSLEY

½ cup/55 g coarsely grated PARMIGIANO-REGGIANO (I use a food processor; see p. 212.)

TOASTED GARLIC BREAD CRUMBS (recipe follows)

{Stovetop Pastas} Lovely lime-colored Broccoflower had me from hello. It wasn't just the color that got me; I loved the flavor and texture and the way it caramelizes, too. I was so enchanted, in fact, that I didn't even realize that Broccoflower is the trademark of California produce company Tanimura & Antle. Virtually the same vegetable may be in your store labeled "green cauliflower." Broccoflower, or green cauliflower, does have a bit of broccoli in the genes, and the texture is slightly firmer and the flavor a tad sweeter than cauliflower. It cooks a bit more quickly, too, which is why I don't necessarily recommend substituting cauliflower in this recipe—unless you are comfortable lengthening the initial browning time and the final simmer. I love the garlicky, lemony, sauce for this dish, which was inspired by a favorite side dish in *Fast, Fresh & Green*. Cut florets on the small side for this pasta, and don't be afraid to let them brown up quite a bit for the best flavor. Finish the dish with a garnish of crispy, toasty, bread crumbs, and this makes a satisfying meal in a bowl.

SERVES 3

1 ***In a glass measure,*** combine the lemon juice, lemon zest, honey, and mustard. Set aside.

2 ***Bring a large pot of salted water to a boil.*** Put a colander in the sink and place a glass liquid measure next to it. Add the orecchiette to the boiling water and cook until al dente, about 11 minutes, or according to the package instructions. Take the pot off the heat and, before draining the pasta, ladle or pour ½ cup/120 ml of the pasta water into the glass measure. Drain the pasta in the colander and let sit, loosely covered with foil or a pot lid.

3 ***Add the pasta water*** to the lemon-mustard mixture and stir well.

4 ***In a large nonstick stir-fry pan,*** heat 2 tbsp of the butter and the olive oil over medium-high heat. When the butter has melted, add the Broccoflower, onion, and 1¼ tsp salt and toss well. Cook, stirring occasionally (but not too frequently) at first and a little more frequently when browning begins, until the onion is limp and very well browned and all the Broccoflower has browning on it, about 15 minutes. Add the garlic and cook, stirring, just until fragrant, about 30 seconds.

5 ***Reduce the heat to medium,*** pour in the lemon–pasta water mixture, and stir. Cover (use a baking sheet if you don't have a lid) and cook for about 2 minutes (no longer), just to finish the Broccoflower and to reduce the sauce slightly. Remove the pan from the heat and add the cold butter, a few pieces at a time, stirring until it melts and becomes creamy. Add the drained pasta to the pan and season it with ¼ tsp salt and several grinds of pepper. Add most of the parsley and most of the Parmigiano. Stir everything until well combined.

6 ***Serve right away,*** garnished with the remaining parsley and Parmigiano and the bread crumbs.

Toasted Garlic Bread Crumbs

I like to make these close to serving time, but you can certainly make them up to 2 hours ahead. Cover the plate loosely and keep at room temperature.

1 tbsp **UNSALTED BUTTER**

1 tsp **MINCED GARLIC**

¾ cup/52 g **COARSE FRESH BREAD CRUMBS** (I like English muffins; see page 212.)

KOSHER SALT

In a small nonstick skillet, melt the butter over medium-low heat. Add the garlic and cook, stirring, until it has softened and is fragrant, about 30 seconds. (Do not brown.) Add the bread crumbs and a small pinch of salt and cook, stirring with a silicone spatula, until well combined. Continue to cook, stirring, until the crumbs are lightly toasted and golden brown, 5 to 6 minutes. (It may be hard to see the browning in a nonstick skillet. The crumbs will feel lighter and crisper.) Remove the pan from the heat and transfer the crumbs to a plate to cool. **MAKES A SCANT ¾ CUP**

Spaghetti

with Roasted Cherry Tomatoes & Spicy Garlic Oil for Two

- 3 tbsp **EXTRA-VIRGIN OLIVE OIL**
- 1 tbsp minced **GARLIC**
- Scant ½ tsp **CRUSHED RED PEPPER FLAKES**
- **KOSHER SALT**
- 6 oz/170 g **DRIED SPAGHETTI**
- **ROASTED CHERRY TOMATOES** (page 91)
- ¼ cup/30 g coarsely grated **PARMIGIANO-REGGIANO**
- 2 tbsp thinly sliced **FRESH BASIL** or **MINT LEAVES**, or a combination of the two, plus more (if desired).

{Stovetop Pastas} This is our go-to weeknight pasta not only in summer, when our cherry tomato plants are exploding (we love black cherries, especially), but in winter, too, when cherries are a better bet than many larger tomatoes. Roasting intensifies their flavor (I also use these in bread pudding, see page 89), and the rest of the pasta comes together so quickly that I don't mind the 30 minutes or so that the tomatoes spend in the oven. (Yes, I'm cheating a bit here; this pasta isn't entirely made on the stovetop. But you'll forgive me when you taste it.) The other flavor secret here is infused oil, which my Boston-chef friend Tony Rosenfeld, who learned to cook great pasta in Rome, taught me. I use the olive oil, simmered with garlic and crushed red pepper, as the "sauce" for the spaghetti. When I fold in the roasted cherry tomatoes, they add just enough juice to lend the spaghetti a lovely color and extra flavor. Lots of fresh basil and a little Parmigiano, and dinner is served—with Grilled Bread (page 203), naturally.

SERVES 2

1 ***In a small nonstick skillet,*** heat the olive oil over medium-low heat. Add the garlic and red pepper and cook, stirring, until the garlic begins to simmer in the oil. Cook for just about 30 seconds more to infuse the oil. (Do not let the garlic brown.) Remove the skillet from the heat and set aside. (Do not transfer the contents to a bowl.)

2 ***Bring a large pot of salted water to a boil.*** Put a colander in the sink and place a small cup next to it. Add the spaghetti to the boiling water and cook until al dente, about 7 minutes, or according to the package instructions. Take the pot off the heat and, before draining the pasta, pour 2 to 3 tbsp of the pasta water into the cup. Drain the pasta in the colander and return it to the pot.

3 ***Gently reheat the infused oil,*** if necessary.

4 ***Season the pasta with ¼ tsp salt*** and drizzle and scrape all the spicy garlic oil over it. Toss well. Add the roasted cherry tomatoes, Parmigiano, and 1 to 2 tbsp of the pasta water. Stir gently but thoroughly until the pasta turns a light pink color. (You don't want to break up the tomatoes, just release a bit of their juice.) Stir in most of the basil. Using tongs, divide the spaghetti and the roasted tomatoes between two shallow serving bowls.

5 ***Garnish with the remaining basil*** and serve right away.

Gemelli

with Buttery Leeks, Baby Spinach & Tender Mushrooms

- 2 tbsp freshly squeezed ORANGE JUICE
- 2 tbsp HEAVY CREAM
- KOSHER SALT
- 3 tbsp UNSALTED BUTTER
- 2 tbsp EXTRA-VIRGIN OLIVE OIL
- 2 cups/200 g thickly sliced LEEKS (white and light green parts only from about 5 or 6 small leeks or 3 or 4 large, leeks, washed thoroughly)
- 8 oz/225 g CREMINI or BABY BELLA MUSHROOMS, halved and thickly sliced
- ½ lb/225 g DRIED GEMELLI
- 2 tsp minced GARLIC
- 1 tsp minced peeled FRESH GINGER
- 5 oz/140 g BABY SPINACH LEAVES
- FRESHLY GROUND PEPPER
- ½ cup/55 g coarsely grated PARMIGIANO-REGGIANO
- 2 tbsp chopped FRESH PARSLEY (optional)

{Stovetop Pastas} Some days I think leeks may be my favorite vegetable. (Okay, so that designation changes about as frequently as the wind direction—which is pretty often here on blustery Martha's Vineyard!). But, really, I do think this allium is underappreciated. It has an incredibly deep, earthy flavor and a buttery texture when cooked down that can lend depth to any number of dishes. I've used leeks as the backbone for this comforting pasta, which also includes mushrooms, spinach, a bit of garlic, a touch of ginger, and a very light "cream" sauce (which incorporates some of the pasta cooking water). Despite using my favorite stir-fry pan again here, I don't cook these veggies quickly. I let them simmer in their own juices first; then, when the juices reduce, the veggies have developed a soft texture and deep flavor that's perfect for a creamy pasta. Because the veggies take a little longer to cook than the pasta, get your pasta water boiling, but don't drop the pasta in until you've started cooking your veggies. Be sure to season this pasta generously with freshly ground pepper.

SERVES 3 GENEROUSLY

1 *In a glass measure,* combine the orange juice and cream. Set aside.

2 *Bring a large pot of salted water to a boil.* Put a colander in the sink and place a glass liquid measure next to it.

3 *Meanwhile, in a large nonstick stir-fry pan,* heat 2 tbsp of the butter and the olive oil over medium-high heat. When the butter has melted, add the leeks, mushrooms, and 1¼ tsp salt. Cook, stirring occasionally at first (the veggies will give off water) and a little more frequently when browning begins, until the veggies have shrunk, the leeks are very soft and have collapsed, and the mushrooms are a bit browned, 16 to 18 minutes.

4 *Add the gemelli to the boiling water* and cook until al dente, about 12 minutes, or according to the package instructions. Take the pasta pot off the heat, and before draining the pasta, pour or ladle ⅓ cup/75 ml of the pasta water into the glass measure. Drain the pasta in the colander and let sit, loosely covered with a pot lid or aluminum foil. Add the pasta water to the orange-cream mixture and stir well.

5 *Reduce the heat* under the stir-fry pan to medium and add the remaining 1 tbsp butter, garlic, and ginger. Stir until the aromatics are fragrant, about 30 seconds. Add the spinach and cook, stirring and flipping with tongs, until the spinach is wilted, 1 to 2 minutes. Add the pasta water–cream mixture and bring to a simmer (this will take only a few seconds). Remove the pan from the heat.

6 *Add the drained pasta to the pan* and season it with ¼ tsp salt and several grinds of fresh pepper. Add most of the Parmigiano and stir until very well combined.

7 *Serve right away,* dividing the pasta and the veggies evenly among three bowls. Garnish each with the remaining Parmigiano and the parsley (if using).

Spicy, Garlicky Corkscrew Pasta

with Broccoli, Sun-Dried Tomatoes & Goat Cheese

KOSHER SALT

½ lb/225 g DRIED CAVATAPPI or other CORKSCREW-SHAPED PASTA

5 tbsp/75 ml EXTRA-VIRGIN OLIVE OIL, plus more if needed

1 tbsp minced GARLIC

¼ tsp CRUSHED RED PEPPER FLAKES

1 pound/455 g small BROCCOLI FLORETS (from about 4 crowns), cut into pieces about 1 to 1¼ in/ 2.5 to 3 cm long and ½ to ¾ in/ 12 mm to 2 cm wide

½ cup/70 g thinly sliced drained OIL-PACKED SUN-DRIED TOMATOES

2 oz/55 g GOAT CHEESE, crumbled while still cold

⅓ cup/40 g) coarsely grated PARMIGIANO-REGGIANO (I use a food processor; see page 212.)

{Stovetop Pastas} Broccoli loves garlic. And spicy crushed red pepper flakes. And tangy sun-dried tomatoes. And creamy goat cheese. And pasta. It's as simple and delicious as that—a classic pasta combination. The difference here is the big flavor boost the broccoli gets from being browned in a stir-fry pan (which conveniently takes about the same time as it does to cook the pasta). Plus, the pasta itself gets a boost, from a quickly infused garlic-and-crushed-pepper olive oil. (If you like things spicy, up the red pepper from ¼ to ½ tsp.) Lastly, I use the pasta cooking water again in this pasta to finish cooking the broccoli and to loosen the goat cheese. Try to keep the broccoli florets on the small side, so they'll all cook together in about 10 minutes.

SERVES 3 GENEROUSLY

1 ***Bring a large pot of salted water to a boil.*** Put a colander in the sink and place a glass liquid measure next to it. Add the pasta to the boiling water and cook until al dente, 9 to 10 minutes, or according to the package instructions. Take the pot off the heat and, before draining the pasta, ladle or pour about 2/3 cup/165 ml of the pasta water into the glass measure. Drain the pasta in the colander and let it sit, loosely covered with foil or a pot lid.

2 ***Have ready a small heatproof bowl*** near the stove. In a large nonstick stir-fry pan, heat 3 tbsp of the olive oil over medium-low heat. When the oil is hot, add the garlic and red pepper flakes and cook, stirring, until the garlic begins to simmer in the oil. Cook for just about 30 seconds more to infuse the oil. (Do not let the garlic brown.) Pour and scrape all the seasoned oil into the heatproof bowl and reserve. Wipe the pan out with a paper towel.

⟶

3 ***Return the pan to the heat,*** add the remaining 2 tbsp olive oil, and raise the heat to medium-high. When the oil is hot (it will loosen up), add the broccoli and 1 tsp salt and stir well. (I like a silicone spoonula for this.) The pan will seem crowded and the broccoli may look dry, but don't worry; the broccoli will shrink and give off moisture as it cooks. Cook, stirring occasionally, until the broccoli has shrunk (it will mostly fit in a single layer in the pan), all the florets have turned bright green, and most have a little browning on them, about 10 minutes.

4 ***Measure out 1/3 cup/75 ml of the pasta water*** (save the rest) and pour it into the stir-fry pan. Quickly add the sun-dried tomatoes. Then cover the pan briefly (if you don't have a lid, improvise with a sheet pan) and continue cooking until the water has simmered down to almost nothing (this will happen in just 15 to 20 seconds). Uncover and remove the pan from the heat.

5 ***Add the drained pasta to the pan,*** season it with 1/4 tsp salt, and drizzle it with all the reserved garlic–red pepper oil. (Be sure to scrape all the seasoned oil out of the bowl.) Stir briefly. Add all of the goat cheese and most of the Parmigiano and stir until everything is well distributed. Add another 1 to 2 tbsp pasta water and stir again until the goat cheese loosens up a bit and gets creamier. Add another 1 to 2 tbsp pasta water, if necessary.

6 ***Serve right away,*** garnished with the remaining Parmigiano.

Greek Spinach-Salad Pasta

with Feta, Olives, Artichokes, Tomatoes & Pepperoncini

{Cool Pastas} I once watched 200 lb/90 kg of Greek pasta salad fly out the door of a take-out market one Fourth of July weekend. It was a popular dish we made, and it always sold well, but that blew me away! These days, I make a quick and colorful Greek pasta that isn't exactly a salad: I like to toss the warm pasta with the marinated vegetables and fresh spinach to make a more sophisticated room-temperature pasta dish. But it does have all the bright flavors of a great Greek salad, including lemon, olives, garlic, fresh oregano, red onions, artichoke hearts, grape tomatoes, and feta cheese. Everything goes in raw except the pasta, so the timing is easy: Prep ahead, then cook the pasta when you're ready to eat. For fun add a few tangy pepperoncini. You don't have to include them, but they add a nice spark. (Buy them whole, not sliced.) This pasta is perfect for a summer supper and is plenty filling for vegetarians. But it would be lovely with grilled swordfish or shrimp skewers, too.

SERVES 5 OR 6

¼ cup/60 ml mild EXTRA-VIRGIN OLIVE OIL

1 tbsp plus 1 tsp WHITE BALSAMIC VINEGAR

2 tsp chopped GARLIC

2 tsp finely grated LEMON ZEST

1 tsp BLACK OLIVE TAPENADE

1 tsp HONEY

KOSHER SALT

FRESHLY GROUND PEPPER

1 small RED ONION (about 4 oz/115 g), cut lengthwise into very thin slices

One 14-oz/400-g can ARTICHOKE HEARTS, drained and each heart cut lengthwise into 4 or 6 pieces

8 oz/225 g small GRAPE TOMATOES, halved (about 1¾ cups)

½ cup/85 g pitted KALAMATA OLIVES, quartered lengthwise

4 oz/115 g good-quality CREAMY FETA CHEESE (I like French Valbreso), crumbled

2 tbsp chopped FRESH OREGANO

8 oz/225 g DRIED GEMELLI or other curly pasta

4 oz/115 g BABY SPINACH LEAVES (about 5 cups)

⅓ cup/35 g chopped TOASTED WALNUTS (page 198)

12 to 16 small whole PEPPERONCINI, drained (about 2 oz/55 g)

1 ***In a large, wide mixing bowl,*** whisk or stir together the olive oil, vinegar, garlic, lemon zest, tapenade, honey, ½ tsp salt, and several grinds of pepper. Add the red onion, artichoke hearts, grape tomatoes, olives, feta, and 1 tbsp of the oregano and toss well. Let the mixture sit for 15 to 20 minutes.

2 ***Bring a large pot of well-salted water to a boil.*** Add the gemelli and cook until al dente, about 12 minutes, or according to the package instructions. Drain well in a colander but do not rinse. Transfer the warm pasta to the mixing bowl with the dressing and vegetables and season with ¼ tsp salt. Add the spinach leaves, the remaining 1 tbsp of oregano, the toasted walnuts, and the pepperoncini and toss well. (The feta will loosen up and coat the pasta.) Taste and season with more salt and pepper, if desired. (You can also let the tossed pasta sit for a few minutes, stir again, and taste.)

3 ***Serve right away.***

Peanut Noodles

with Spring Veggies & Whole-Wheat Linguine

FOR THE SAUCE

1 large GARLIC CLOVE

1 piece (about 1¼ in/3.5 cm square) FRESH GINGER, peeled and sliced

⅓ cup/15 g packed FRESH CILANTRO LEAVES

¾ cup/190 g CREAMY PEANUT BUTTER

⅓ cup/75 ml LOW-SODIUM SOY SAUCE

1 tbsp plus 2 tsp freshly squeezed LEMON JUICE

1 tbsp PEANUT OIL

1 tbsp ASIAN SESAME OIL

2 tsp SUGAR

¾ tsp ASIAN CHILI-GARLIC SAUCE

FOR THE PASTA

1 lb/445 g WHOLE-WHEAT DRIED LINGUINE

KOSHER SALT

1 tsp PEANUT OIL

3 oz/85 g SNOW PEAS, trimmed and cut on a sharp diagonal into very thin slices (about 1 cup)

3½ oz/100 g SUGAR SNAP PEAS, trimmed and cut on the diagonal into thin slices (about 1 cup)

3 oz/85 g CARROTS, very thinly sliced (matchsticks) or coarsely grated (about 1 cup)

{Cool Pastas} This cool pasta takes advantage of an easy food-processor peanut sauce that has such a knockout flavor that I often use it as a dip. Here I pair it with whole-wheat noodles and lots of colorful raw veggies like snap peas, carrots, and red cabbage for a big crowd-pleasing pasta dish. You can take this along to a summer picnic or potluck or serve it as the main event for supper with grilled chicken thighs on the side. It looks really pretty in a big bowl, garnished with some of the veggies and lots of chopped fresh cilantro and roasted peanuts. You can make the sauce a day ahead. (Let it come to room temperature before using, and thin with a little hot water, if necessary.) A small or large food processor will work for blending the sauce; if you don't have either, a blender will work as long as you pre-chop the garlic, ginger, and cilantro. Also feel free to change up the veggies if you like (broccoli, peppers, or beans work, too). Just keep them thinly sliced or small-diced.

SERVES 6

1 ***To make the sauce:*** In a food processor, chop the garlic, ginger, and cilantro, stopping to scrape down the sides of the bowl as necessary to chop thoroughly. Scrape the bowl and add the peanut butter, soy sauce, lemon juice, peanut oil, sesame oil, sugar, and chili-garlic sauce. Process until well combined, scraping the bowl as necessary. Add ½ cup/120 ml hot water and process until the mixture is creamy and well mixed, 1 to 2 minutes. Transfer the sauce (scraping the bowl well) to a 2-cup/480-ml liquid measure or other sturdy, deep bowl.

2½ oz/70 g thinly sliced RED CABBAGE (about 1 cup)

⅔ cup/55 g thinly sliced SCALLIONS (whites and most of the greens from one bunch)

⅓ cup/10 g chopped FRESH CILANTRO

⅓ cup/45 g finely chopped ROASTED PEANUTS

½ cup/10 g BEAN SPROUTS (optional)

2 ***To make the pasta:*** Cook the linguine according to the package instructions in well-salted boiling water. Transfer to a colander, rinse with cool water, and let drain for several minutes. Transfer to a large mixing bowl. Add the peanut oil and 1 tsp salt and mix well.

3 ***Add most of the snow peas,*** snap peas, carrots, cabbage, scallions, and cilantro to the bowl with the pasta, reserving a little of each for garnish.

4 ***Pour three-quarters of the sauce*** over the vegetables and pasta and, using tongs, gently but thoroughly toss well. Taste and continue to add more sauce, 2 to 3 tbsp at a time, until the noodles are well coated. (You may have a little sauce left over.) Taste and season with a little more salt (if desired).

5 ***Transfer the dressed noodles*** and vegetables to a large shallow serving bowl. Garnish with the remaining vegetables and cilantro as well as the roasted peanuts and bean sprouts (if using) before serving.

Classic Baked Pasta

with Roasted Tomato Sauce for Two

{Baked Pastas} Pizza to pasta—that's the route my red sauce traveled. Once I puréed tasty roasted plum tomatoes to make a pizza sauce, I realized how delicious that same sauce would be on pasta, too. (It's all about the tomatoes.) Now, when I think of it, I make lots of this yummy stuff and freeze it. Then I use it to make a super-quick and simple baked pasta for two of us on a weeknight. (The rest of the ingredient list is super-short, and the pasta only takes 20 minutes to bake.) I have a 1½-qt/1.4-L gratin dish that's just the right size for this pasta, but I've also found that a square heatproof glass pan or pie plate works fine, too. For individual pastas, use two 3-cup/720-ml baking dishes. If you want to change it up, replace the mushrooms with another veggie like broccoli, peas, or fennel. (Or add a little sausage or ground beef, if you like.) With crusty bread and a green salad (see page 182), dinner is on.

SERVES 2

→

EXTRA-VIRGIN OLIVE OIL

1 cup/240 ml QUICK-ROASTED PLUM TOMATO PIZZA SAUCE (page 167)

KOSHER SALT

4 oz/115 g SHAPED DRIED PASTA OF YOUR CHOICE (I like CAVATAPPI and CAMPANELLE.)

4 oz/115 g diced FRESH MOZZARELLA (about 1 medium ball or ½ large ball)

6 tbsp/40 g coarsely grated PARMIGIANO-REGGIANO (see page 212)

1½ tbsp chopped FRESH MINT, BASIL, PARSLEY, or any combination of the three, or 1 to 2 tsp FRESH THYME, OREGANO, or a combination of the two

4 oz/115 g FRESH MUSHROOMS, sliced and sautéed in olive oil until shrunken and golden brown

1 ***Preheat the oven to 450°F/230°C/gas 8.*** Brush a 1½-qt/1.4-L shallow gratin or other similar-size baking dish with olive oil. Put the tomato sauce in a medium mixing bowl.

2 ***Bring a large saucepan of water to a boil*** and add 1 tsp salt. Add the pasta to the boiling water and cook until al dente, or according to the package instructions. Before draining, add 3 tbsp of the pasta cooking water to the tomato sauce and whisk to thin the sauce slightly. Drain the pasta well in a colander and transfer it to the bowl of sauce. Sprinkle it with ¼ tsp salt. Add the mozzarella, 3 tbsp of the Parmigiano, the herbs, and the mushrooms to the pasta and stir well.

3 ***Transfer the pasta mixture*** to the prepared baking dish, spreading it in an even layer. Top with the remaining 3 tbsp Parmigiano. Bake until brown and bubbly, about 20 minutes. Let cool for a minute or two and serve hot.

Baked Penne

with Silky Fennel in Hot Pink Sauce

2 tbsp **UNSALTED BUTTER**, plus more for the baking dish

3/4 cup/50 g **FRESH BREAD CRUMBS**

3/4 cup/85 g coarsely grated **PARMIGIANO-REGGIANO**

2 tsp **EXTRA-VIRGIN OLIVE OIL**, plus 2 tbsp

KOSHER SALT

3 tbsp chopped **FRESH PARSLEY**

1/2 cup/120 ml plus 2 tbsp **HEAVY CREAM**

1/2 lb/225 g **DRIED PENNE RIGATE**

2 **FENNEL BULBS** (about 1 1/4 lb/570 g each with stalks)

1 tbsp minced **GARLIC**

1/4 tsp **CRUSHED RED PEPPER FLAKES**

2 tbsp **VODKA**

3/4 cup/180 ml **CRUSHED TOMATOES** without herbs (I like Cento brand.)

8 oz/225 g diced **FRESH MOZZARELLA**

{Baked Pastas} This I eat straight out of the pan. Well, I wait just a few minutes for it to stop bubbling after it comes out of the oven. But then I'm in. Stand back. Seriously, there is plenty here to share—four can feast on this pasta, in which a luscious "hot" pink sauce stars. The sauce is based on a generous amount of fresh fennel that's been sautéed until meltingly sweet and brown. A splash of vodka, a bit of crushed red pepper, and a combination of crushed tomatoes, cream, and pasta cooking water all go into the fennel pot to wash up all those yummy browned bits from the bottom of the pan. The result is a sauce with fabulous flavor. (And one that makes a good introduction to fennel for folks who are unfamiliar with it.) With plenty of fresh mozzarella and Parmigiano, plus a crisp bread crumb topping, this is a rich one, I'll admit. But paired with the cooling Winter Green & White Salad (page 195) and some good crusty ciabatta, this makes for a memorable Friday night dinner with friends.

SERVES 4

1 ***Preheat the oven to 425°F/220°C/gas 7.*** Rub a 13-by-9-in/33-by-23-cm shallow baking dish with a little bit of the butter. In a small bowl, combine the bread crumbs, 1/4 cup of the Parmigiano, the 2 tsp olive oil, a pinch of salt, and 2 tsp of the parsley and mix well.

2 ***Pour the cream*** into a 2-cup/480-ml glass measure.

3 ***Bring a large pot of salted water to a boil.*** Put a colander in the sink, and place a glass liquid measure next to it. Add the penne to the boiling water and cook until al dente, or according to the package instructions. Take the pot off the heat and, before draining the pasta, pour or ladle 3/4 cup/180 ml of the pasta cooking water into the glass measure. Drain the pasta in the colander and set aside. Add the reserved pasta water to the heavy cream.

4 ***Trim the stalks from the fennel.*** Trim any brown spots from the outside of the fennel and halve the bulb. Cut most of the core from both halves, leaving a bit of it to hold some of the wedges together (some will naturally fall apart into slices). Cut the fennel lengthwise (rotating your knife as you go, so that you are cutting on a radial angle always toward the center) into 1/4-in-/6-mm-thick wedges or slices. (You should have about 5 1/2 cups/570 g thinly sliced fennel.)

5 ***In a large Dutch oven*** or other deep, wide pot, heat the 2 tbsp butter and 2 tbsp olive oil over medium-high heat. When the butter has melted, add the fennel and 1 tsp salt. Cover and cook, stirring frequently (tongs are easiest for tossing and turning), until the fennel is very tender and well browned, 12 to 14 minutes. (The bottom of the pot may be browning quite a bit. That's okay; just be sure to stir almost constantly toward the end of cooking and, as you stir, rub the fennel against the tasty brown spots to help dislodge them. Reduce the heat to medium if browning is going a bit too quickly.)

6 ***Reduce the heat to medium-low,*** add the garlic and crushed red pepper, and cook, stirring, until fragrant, about 30 seconds. Add the vodka and cook, stirring and scraping the bottom of the pot, while it simmers down (this will take just a few seconds). Add the crushed tomatoes and cook, stirring and scraping the bottom of the pot, until well mixed, about 30 seconds. Add the cream–pasta water mixture and cook, stirring well, for 30 seconds to 1 minute. Remove the pot from the heat.

7 ***Add the penne to the pot,*** season it with 1/4 tsp salt, and stir. Add the mozzarella, the remaining Parmigiano, and the remaining parsley and stir well. Pour and scrape the mixture into the prepared baking dish and spread evenly with a spatula. You may have to move the ingredients around a bit and press down with the spatula to ensure that the pasta is well distributed. Sprinkle the bread crumb mixture evenly over the top.

8 ***Bake until the top is browned*** and crusty, the casserole is bubbling vigorously, and the juices have bubbled down a bit, leaving a brown ring on the inside of the pan, about 25 minutes. Let sit for a few minutes while the bubbling subsides and then serve right away.

Hearty Baked Pasta

with Roasted Eggplant, Mushrooms, Peppers & Thyme

- 1 small EGGPLANT (about 12 oz/340 g), peeled and cut into ½- to ¾-in/12-mm to 2-cm dice
- 4 oz/115 g CREMINI or BABY BELLA MUSHROOMS, quartered if small, cut into 6 pieces if larger
- 1 small RED or YELLOW BELL PEPPER (5 oz/140 g), cut into ½- to ¾-in/12-mm to 2-cm dice
- KOSHER SALT
- 4 tbsp plus 2 tsp EXTRA-VIRGIN OLIVE OIL
- BUTTER for the baking dish
- ¾ cup/50 g FRESH BREAD CRUMBS (I like to use English muffins; see page 212.)
- ¾ cup/85 g coarsely grated PARMIGIANO-REGGIANO
- 1 tbsp chopped FRESH THYME
- ⅓ cup/75 ml HEAVY CREAM
- 3 tbsp DRY RED WINE
- 1 tsp BALSAMIC VINEGAR
- ½ lb/225 g SMALL SHAPED DRIED PASTA such as CAMPANELLE, CAVATAPPI, or MEDIUM SHELLS
- 1 medium ONION, diced (about 1⅓ cups)
- 1 tbsp plus 1 tsp minced GARLIC

{Baked Pastas} We love baked pasta in our house: I love to cook it, and we all love to eat it, with that melty mozzarella doing its ooey-gooey-stretchy thing. Even this vegetarian baked pasta gets the thumbs-up from our meat lovers, because it's so hearty. It features roasted eggplant, mushrooms, and bell peppers, which I think is a good all-season combo. But I've made this with roasted squash and shallots, with a trio of different mushrooms, and with other veggies, too, and they've all been delicious. If you want to experiment, just start with 1 lb/455 g of raw veggies, and you'll be fine. (You could also slip in a little meat, if you like, though this pasta is plenty satisfying without it.) One tip: Before using canned crushed tomatoes, taste them. Brands vary significantly, and some are rather bad (sour or overly acidic); you should cook with one you find acceptable straight out of the can. Avoid those with basil or other herbs added to them.

SERVES 4

1 ***Preheat the oven to 450°F/230°C/gas 8.*** Line a large, heavy-duty, rimmed baking sheet with parchment. In a medium mixing bowl, combine the eggplant, mushrooms, and bell pepper. Season with 1 tsp salt, drizzle with 3 tbsp of the olive oil, and toss to coat well. Transfer the vegetables to the prepared baking sheet and spread in a single layer. Roast until the vegetables are tender, shrunken, and browned, 26 to 30 minutes. Let cool on the baking sheet.

2 ***Reduce the oven temperature to 425°F/220°C/gas 7.*** Rub a 13-by-9-in/33-by-23-cm shallow baking dish with some butter. In a small bowl, combine the bread crumbs, 1/4 cup/30 g of the Parmigiano, 2 tsp of the olive oil, 1/4 tsp of the thyme, and a pinch of salt and mix well.

3 ***Pour the cream*** into a 2-cup/480-ml glass measure and put it near the sink. In a small bowl, combine the red wine and balsamic vinegar.

¼ tsp CRUSHED RED PEPPER FLAKES

1¼ cups/300 ml CRUSHED TOMATOES without herbs (I like Cento brand.)

½ lb/225 g diced FRESH MOZZARELLA

4 ***Bring a large pot of salted water to a boil.*** Put a colander in the sink and place a glass liquid measure next to it. Add the pasta to the boiling water and cook it until al dente, about 10 minutes, or according to the package instructions. Take the pot off the heat and, before draining the pasta, pour or ladle 1 cup/240 ml of the pasta water into the glass measure. Drain the pasta in the colander and set aside. Add the reserved pasta water to the cream.

5 ***In a deep skillet or Dutch oven,*** heat the remaining 1 tbsp olive oil over medium-low heat. When the oil is hot, add the onion and a pinch of salt. Cover and cook, stirring occasionally, until softened and lightly browned, about 10 minutes. Uncover, add the minced garlic and crushed red pepper, and cook, stirring, until fragrant, about 30 seconds. Add the red wine–balsamic mixture to the pan, and cook, stirring, while it simmers down, 30 to 60 seconds.

6 ***Add the crushed tomatoes*** and cook, stirring, for about 1 minute. Add the cream–pasta water mixture, stir well, and bring to a simmer. Cook for 30 seconds and remove the pan from the heat.

7 ***Add the pasta to the sauce,*** season it with ¼ tsp salt, and stir. Add the roasted vegetables, mozzarella, remaining Parmigiano, and remaining thyme and stir well. Pour and scrape the mixture into the baking dish and spread evenly. Top with the bread-crumb mixture.

8 ***Bake until the top is browned*** and crusty and the juices have bubbled down a bit, leaving a brown ring on the inside of the pan, 25 to 28 minutes. Serve right away.

CHAPTER 4

EGGS (+ VEGGIES) FOR DINNER

Making Eggs (+ Veggies) for Dinner: How It Works

Full disclosure: I have fallen in love with eggs. And it looks like it's an affair that won't be ending any time soon. I didn't like eggs as a kid. (Well, I didn't like much of anything, really, other than candy.) But during a particularly stressful time in my adult life, I began to eat a lot of them and noticed how satisfying they were—no shallow calories here. Then I moved to the Vineyard and the second day I was here (literally), I was introduced to a barnyard of hens and their multihued eggs. Inside those pretty eggs were plump marigold yolks that reminded me of drawings in our kindergarten storybooks! Turns out those eggs cook up extra fluffy and taste like sunrise. I was hooked. (Now I've got my own hens, too.)

But you needn't have farm-fresh eggs to make delicious egg dishes. Truth is, eggs (all eggs!) and veggies were made for each other. The two partner so beautifully that I could eat something like my Fresh Corn, Zucchini, Onion & Basil Frittata every night.

I'd never cooked a frittata (basically a giant skillet omelet) until my first cooking job at Al Forno restaurant in Providence, Rhode Island, years ago. There I had to make one every night for the antipasto plate, and I quickly learned which veggies worked best: nothing watery, nothing raw; again, anything sautéed or roasted first to shed excess water and gain flavor was best.

I also learned the easiest technique for making a frittata. Forget any rumors of scary flipping. Here's all you do: Whisk up the custard, veggie, and cheese mixture in a big bowl; heat a combo of butter and olive oil in a heavy skillet; pour and scrape the mixture in; and let it brown for a minute on the bottom. Pop the skillet in a hot oven, then wait for it to get golden and puffy, about 25 minutes. You'll just need a heavy-duty 10-in/25-cm ovenproof nonstick skillet for the best results with these recipes.

At my next job I learned the wonder of a seriously silky custard. (I made quiche every day.) I've used that custard here in my savory bread puddings. These baked egg/bread dishes are similar to stratas, only they have a more delicate texture, achieved by the right proportion of heavy cream and eggs, and, in my case, the choice of a fine-textured bread like challah. Despite the rich ingredients, "pudding" is a bit of a misnomer as these actually wind up feeling light and almost soufflélike. Savory bread puddings are the perfect showcase for leafy greens (like my favorite, Tuscan kale) as well as for spring veggies like asparagus and peas. Summer veggies, too. Did I mention that corn is my favorite veg with eggs? And wait till you try the bread pudding with roasted cherry tomatoes!

Two important things about flavoring eggs: Season them well before cooking to bring out their best flavor. (Salt the custard just before cooking.) Also, be generous (think tbsp and quarter cups) with tender fresh herbs. Eggs love cilantro—and mint, basil, and chives, too.

Fresh Corn, Zucchini, Onion & Basil Frittata

2 tbsp UNSALTED BUTTER

1 tbsp EXTRA-VIRGIN OLIVE OIL

1 medium YELLOW ONION, finely diced (1½ cups)

KOSHER SALT

1 medium-small ZUCCHINI or other summer squash, finely diced (1¼ cups)

2 cups/315 g FRESH CORN KERNELS, cut from about 3 large or 4 small ears **(see page 213)**

7 large EGGS, preferably free-range and ideally at room temperature

⅓ cup/75 ml WHOLE MILK

⅓ cup/75 ml HEAVY CREAM

FRESHLY GROUND PEPPER

½ cup/55 g coarsely grated PARMIGIANO-REGGIANO (I use the food processor, **see page 212.)**

½ cup/60 g packaged grated MOZZARELLA

2 tbsp chopped FRESH BASIL

1 tbsp chopped FRESH CILANTRO

{Frittatas} As I mentioned, my very favorite vegetable with eggs is fresh corn. If you've never had an omelet or a frittata with juicy, sweet, fresh corn kernels in it, you will have to take my word for it . . . until you try this, my (not surprisingly) favorite fritatta. Eggs are also one of the absolute best destinations for fresh herbs in summertime, so a classic combo of corn, zucchini, and basil (with a nice hit of sweet sautéed onions) makes this a perfect late-August meal. It's very filling, too, so a quick salad of arugula tossed with lemon and scallions and a slice of crusty artisan bread with olive oil would be a lovely way to round out the meal. Please do not used canned or frozen corn in this! Leftovers are great at room temperature for breakfast or lunch.

SERVES 4

1 ***Preheat the oven to 375°F/190°C/gas 5.*** Position a rack in the center of the oven.

2 ***In a 10-in/25-cm heavy nonstick ovenproof skillet,*** heat 1 tbsp of the butter and the olive oil over medium-low heat. When the butter has melted, add the onion and a pinch of salt, cover, and cook, stirring occasionally, until the onion is translucent, about 5 minutes. Uncover, raise the heat to medium, and continue to cook, stirring frequently, until the onion is light golden, another 3 to 4 minutes. Raise the heat to medium-high, add the zucchini and a pinch of salt, and cook, stirring only occasionally, until the zucchini is tender and starting to lose its opacity, another 3 to 4 minutes. Add the remaining 1 tbsp of butter, the corn, and 1/2 tsp salt. Cook, stirring occasionally, until the corn kernels are glistening and some have shrunk slightly, 3 to 4 minutes more. Remove the pan from the heat.

3 ***In a large bowl,*** whisk together the eggs, milk, cream, 1/4 tsp salt, and several grinds of pepper. Add the Parmigiano, mozzarella, basil, and cilantro and whisk again until well combined.

4 ***Return the pan of vegetables*** to medium-high heat and pour and scrape all the custard over them. Using a silicone spatula, gently stir once or twice to move the contents of the pan around so that everything is evenly distributed. Let the pan sit on the heat until the custard is just beginning to set all the way around the edge of the pan, 1 to 2 minutes. Transfer the pan to the preheated oven and bake until the frittata is puffed, golden, and set, about 25 minutes.

5 ***Let the frittata cool*** in the pan for 15 to 20 minutes. Shake the pan a bit to dislodge the frittata and/or run a silicone spatula around the edge of it, slide it onto a cutting board, and let it sit again for a few minutes. (It will stay warm for a while, and the flavor gets better as it sits, so eat it warm or at room temperature.) Cut into quarters or smaller wedges and serve.

Pasta Frittata

with Leeks, Arugula, Goat Cheese & Mint

- **¾ cup/85 g GEMELLI or other small to medium shaped pasta**
- **KOSHER SALT**
- **FRESHLY GROUND PEPPER**
- **2½ tbsp UNSALTED BUTTER**
- **1 tbsp EXTRA-VIRGIN OLIVE OIL, plus 1 tsp**
- **2 cups thinly sliced LEEKS (white and light green parts from about 2 large leeks, about 6 oz/170 g), well washed**
- **1 tsp minced GARLIC**
- **4 oz/115 g BABY ARUGULA LEAVES (about 4 cups packed)**
- **7 large EGGS, preferably free-range and ideally at room temperature**
- **⅓ cup/75 ml WHOLE MILK**
- **⅓ cup/75 ml HEAVY CREAM**
- **⅓ cup/40 g coarsely grated PARMIGIANO-REGGIANO (I use the food processor, see page 212.)**
- **4 oz/110 g cold FRESH GOAT CHEESE, well crumbled while still chilled**
- **1 tbsp finely chopped or thinly sliced FRESH MINT**

{Frittatas} My very first cooking job was at an Italian restaurant where I made the antipasto platter every night. It always had a slice of frittata on the plate (which I'd make during prep time), and the frittata always had pasta in it. Sometimes spaghetti, sometimes shells, but always something that made the frittata not only look lovely but also feel filling. I've made lots of variations since then, but I love this winter-into-spring combo. The sweet sautéed leeks lend an earthy richness, while the tangy goat cheese, arugula, and mint brighten the mix. The flavors come together into one delicious supper that manages to feel both substantial and light at the same time. Be sure to choose a peppy mint and a full-flavored arugula. Taste both before cooking with them, as some grocery store greens can be tasteless. Let this frittata cool a bit before slicing. I think it tastes best warm, not hot, and it keeps on getting tastier as it sits. Leftovers are even better.

SERVES 4

1 ***Preheat the oven to 375°F/190°C/gas 5.*** Position a rack in the center of the oven.

2 ***Cook the gemelli*** in well-salted boiling water according to the package instructions. Drain the pasta well and transfer to a medium bowl. Season with a big pinch of salt and a few grinds of pepper and toss well.

3 ***In a 10-in/25-cm heavy nonstick ovenproof skillet,*** heat 2 tbsp of the butter and the 1 tbsp olive oil over medium-low heat. When the butter has melted, add the leeks and 1/4 tsp salt, cover, and cook, stirring occasionally, until the leeks are softened and translucent, about 5 minutes. Uncover, raise the heat to medium, and continue to cook, stirring frequently, until the leeks have shrunk and browned in places (some more than others), another 8 to 10 minutes. Add the garlic and stir until softened and fragrant, about 30 seconds. Add the arugula to the pan and toss with the leeks until the arugula has completely wilted, about 2 minutes. Transfer the leeks and arugula to the bowl of pasta and toss well. Let cool for 10 minutes. Reserve the skillet.

4 ***In a large bowl,*** whisk the eggs, milk, cream, 1/2 tsp salt, and several grinds of pepper. Stir in the Parmigiano, goat cheese, and mint. Add the pasta mixture and stir well to incorporate all the ingredients.

5 ***Return the skillet to medium-high heat*** and add the remaining 1/2 tbsp butter and 1 tsp olive oil. When the butter has melted and begun to sizzle, pour and scrape all the pasta-custard mixture into the skillet. Using a silicone spatula, gently stir once or twice to move the contents of the pan around so that everything is evenly distributed. Let the pan sit on the heat until the custard is just beginning to set all the way around the edge of the pan, 1 to 2 minutes. Transfer the pan to the preheated oven and bake until the frittata is puffed, golden, and set, about 25 minutes.

6 ***Let the frittata cool*** in the pan for 15 to 20 minutes. Shake the pan a bit to dislodge the frittata and/or run a silicone spatula around the edge of it, slide it onto a cutting board, and let it sit again for a few minutes. (It will stay warm for a while, and the flavor gets better as it sits, so eat it warm or at room temperature.) Cut into quarters or smaller wedges and serve.

Broccoli & Cheddar Frittata

with Red Potatoes & Scallions

½ lb/225 g unpeeled RED POTATOES, cut into small (⅜-in/1-cm) dice

KOSHER SALT

FRESHLY GROUND PEPPER

2½ tbsp UNSALTED BUTTER

½ cup/40 g thinly sliced SCALLIONS (white and as much green part as needed to make ½ cup), plus 3 tbsp thinly sliced green tops

1 tbsp EXTRA-VIRGIN OLIVE OIL, plus 1 tsp

1 BROCCOLI CROWN, cut into small (1-in/2.5-cm) florets (about 3 cups)

7 large EGGS, preferably free-range and ideally at room temperature

⅓ cup/75 ml WHOLE MILK

⅓ cup/75 ml HEAVY CREAM

⅛ tsp WORCESTERSHIRE SAUCE

1½ cups (5½ oz/155 g) EXTRA-SHARP AGED CHEDDAR, coarsely grated

{Frittatas} All the comforts of a baked potato with all the fixin's are right here in one frittata. Well, except the crumbled bacon, though you could certainly add it if you want. One thing I like to do, however, is give the broccoli a flavor boost by sautéing it, not steaming it. Browning the broccoli brings out its intense, nutty side and makes the frittata taste that much more interesting. Choose a very flavorful aged Cheddar, too, and you'll be in business. The funny thing about all frittatas is that they taste better the longer they sit; this one tastes particularly good to me after a night in the fridge. But of course you can still eat it not too long after you make it. It would be great with a cup of Zesty Tomato-Ginger Bisque (page 35).

SERVES 4

1 ***Preheat the oven to 375°F/190°C/gas 5.*** Position a rack in the center of the oven.

2 ***Put the potatoes*** and 1 tsp salt in a medium saucepan, add enough water to cover by 1 in/2.5 cm, and bring to a boil over high heat. Reduce the heat and simmer until tender, about 10 minutes. Drain well and let cool for several minutes. Transfer to a large bowl and season with a pinch of salt and a few grinds of pepper.

3 ***In a 10-in/25-cm heavy nonstick ovenproof skillet,*** melt 1 tbsp of the butter over medium heat. Add the 1/2 cup/40 g scallion slices and cook, stirring occasionally, until softened and starting to brown, 4 to 5 minutes. Transfer to the bowl of potatoes. Return the pan to the heat and add 1 tbsp of the butter and the 1 tbsp olive oil. Raise the heat to medium-high. When the butter has melted, add the broccoli and 1/4 tsp salt. Cover and cook for 2 minutes (the florets will be bright green and starting to brown on the bottom). Uncover and cook, stirring, until the florets are mostly brown on all sides and have lost much (but not all) of their stiffness, 3 to 4 minutes more. Remove from the heat, let cool for a few minutes, and transfer the broccoli to the bowl of potatoes and scallions. Let cool for 5 to 10 minutes. Wipe out the skillet (or rinse it if it has any black spots).

→

4 ***In a large bowl,*** whisk together the eggs, milk, cream, 1/2 tsp salt, Worcestershire sauce, and several grinds of pepper. Stir in the cheese. Add the broccoli mixture and the remaining 3 tbsp scallion tops and stir well.

5 ***Return the skillet to medium-high heat*** and add the remaining 1/2 tbsp butter and 1 tsp olive oil. When the butter has melted and begun to sizzle, pour and scrape all the veggie-custard mixture into the skillet. Using a silicone spatula, gently stir once or twice to move the contents of the pan around so that everything is evenly distributed. Let the pan sit on the heat until the custard is just beginning to set all the way around the edge of the pan, 1 to 2 minutes. Transfer the pan to the preheated oven and bake until the frittata is puffed, golden, and set, about 25 minutes.

6 ***Let the frittata cool*** in the pan for 15 to 20 minutes. Shake the pan a bit to dislodge the frittata and/or run a silicone spatula around the edge of it, slide it onto a cutting board, and let it sit again for a few minutes. (It will stay warm for a while, and the flavor gets better as it sits, so eat it warm or at room temperature.) Cut into quarters or smaller wedges and serve.

Savory Bread Pudding

with Roasted Cherry Tomatoes, Corn & Cilantro

2 tbsp UNSALTED BUTTER, plus more for the baking dish

½ lb/225 g CHALLAH (about ½ loaf), cut into 1-in/2.5-cm cubes

1 tsp minced GARLIC

KOSHER SALT

1 tbsp EXTRA-VIRGIN OLIVE OIL

1 small RED ONION (5 to 6 oz/ 140 to 170 g), cut crosswise into thin slices

8 large EGGS

2 cups/480 ml WHOLE MILK

1 cup/240 ml HEAVY CREAM

½ tsp finely grated LIME ZEST

¼ tsp GROUND CUMIN

¼ tsp GROUND CORIANDER

ROASTED CHERRY TOMATOES (recipe follows)

1 cup/155 g FRESH SWEET CORN, blanched, or FROZEN CORN, thawed (and drained, if necessary)

2 tbsp chopped FRESH CILANTRO

½ cup/55 g coarsely grated MONTEREY JACK

1 cup/85 g coarsely grated AGED CHEDDAR

{Savory Bread Puddings} A savory bread pudding can be just as welcome in late summer or fall as it is in winter, because it's a great destination for summer veggies. In fact, I first made this one after a visit to our farmers' market. (The Orange Peel Bakery sells out of its wonderful challah pretty quickly, but Morning Glory Farm always has plenty of corn.) I can't help using fresh sweet corn in egg dishes (see Fresh Corn, Zucchini, Onion & Basil Frittata, page 82), but in a pinch, you could use frozen corn instead, because the roasted cherry tomatoes are the star here. (They're so good I use them with spaghetti, too. See page 60.) The Southwestern inspiration here provides a secret ingredient—lime zest—that works with the cilantro to impart a surprisingly bright and refreshing flavor to the custard. I like this pudding baked not too long after it's assembled, but like the others, you can hold it in the fridge for up to 2 hours before baking, if you like.

SERVES 6

1 ***Preheat the oven to 375°F/190°C/gas 5.*** Position a rack in the center of the oven. Rub a 13-by-9-in/33-by-23-cm baking dish all over with a little butter.

2 ***Arrange the bread cubes*** in a single layer on a rimmed baking sheet and bake until lightly toasted, 8 to 10 minutes. (They will be starting to turn golden around the edges.) Let the bread cool for a few minutes on the sheet and then transfer them to a large bowl.

3 ***In a small saucepan,*** melt the 2 tbsp butter over medium-low heat. Add the garlic and cook until softened and fragrant, about 1 minute. Scrape and drizzle the butter mixture over the bread cubes, stirring as you drizzle, and toss well. Sprinkle the bread cubes with a little salt and toss again.

4 ***In a medium nonstick skillet,*** heat the olive oil over medium heat. Add the onion and a pinch of salt and cook, stirring, until the onion is limp and browned, about 10 minutes. Set aside.

→

5 ***In a large mixing bowl,*** whisk together the eggs, milk, cream, lime zest, cumin, coriander, and 3/4 tsp salt until well combined.

6 ***Arrange half of the bread cubes*** in a single layer in the prepared baking dish. Top with half of the cherry tomatoes, half of the onion, half of the corn, half of the cilantro, half of the Monterey Jack, and half of the Cheddar. Repeat with the remaining bread, veggies, and cheese. (Be sure to scrape any crumbs or seasoning out of the bread bowl and add them to the pan.) Pour the egg mixture evenly over everything. (Start at one end and pour slowly back and forth.) Using your hands, gently press down on the bread and veggies to force the custard to evenly surround everything. Let sit for about 20 minutes and gently press down again.

7 ***Bake in the preheated oven*** until the bread pudding has risen and is set and dry in the middle (it will be golden all over), about 40 to 45 minutes. Let settle for a few minutes and serve hot or very warm.

Roasted Cherry Tomatoes

For the bread pudding recipe, you can roast these ahead and hold them in the fridge. Choose standard thick-walled cherry tomatoes here; smaller, thinner-skinned tiny tomatoes will not hold up well to roasting.

2 tbsp EXTRA-VIRGIN OLIVE OIL, plus more for the parchment

1 lb/455 g ripe medium red CHERRY TOMATOES, halved

KOSHER SALT

Preheat the oven to 450°F/230°C/gas 8. Line a large heavy-duty rimmed baking sheet with parchment. Brush the parchment with some of the olive oil. Toss the cherry tomato halves very gently with the 2 tbsp olive oil and 1/4 tsp salt and spread in a single layer, cut-side up, on the baking sheet. (Transfer only the tomatoes to the baking sheet, leaving behind any juices in the bowl, as the juices will tend to burn on the baking sheet.) Roast the tomatoes until they are browned around the edges and on the bottom and slightly puckered (they will collapse more when they're out of the oven), about 25 minutes for smaller cherry tomatoes, 32 to 35 minutes for larger ones. (There will be some blackening on the baking sheet.) Let the tomatoes cool somewhat on the sheet. Gently peel them away from the paper. If they are sticking, lift the paper up and pop the tomatoes off by pressing the paper from behind. **MAKES A HEAPING 1 CUP/160 G ROASTED TOMATOES**

Savory Bread Pudding

with Tuscan Kale, Bacon, Scallions & Maple

2 tbsp UNSALTED BUTTER, plus more for the baking dish

½ lb/225 g CHALLAH (about ½ loaf), cut into 1-in/2.5-cm cubes

3 tbsp PURE MAPLE SYRUP

KOSHER SALT

1 bunch (about 10 oz/280 g) TUSCAN KALE, ribs removed and leaves chopped into 1-in/2.5-cm pieces

5 strips BACON, halved to fit in the pan (if necessary)

1 bunch SCALLIONS (white and green parts), cut crosswise into thin slices (about 1 cup/70 g)

8 large EGGS

2 cups/480 ml WHOLE MILK

1 cup/240 ml HEAVY CREAM

½ tsp SHERRY VINEGAR

FRESHLY GROUND PEPPER

½ cup/55 g coarsely grated PARMIGIANO-REGGIANO (I use the food processor; see page 212.)

{Savory Bread Puddings} My favorite leafy green, Tuscan (or lacinato) kale, is the star of this savory bread pudding, which gets a hint of smoky sweetness from two of its favorite flavor partners, bacon and maple. Even though this bread pudding has a bit of meat in it, it still manages to feel light and very pleasing, thanks to the challah and the lovely texture of the custard. The pudding also gets a boost of earthy flavor from sautéed scallions, Parmigiano, and a tiny bit of sherry vinegar. As with the other savory bread puddings in this chapter, there's no need to let the pudding sit for longer than 20 minutes before baking, though you can assemble it ahead and refrigerate it for up to 2 hours before putting it in the oven, if you like.

SERVES 6

1 ***Preheat the oven to 375°F/190°C/gas 5.*** Position a rack in the center of the oven. Rub a 13-by-9-in/33-by-23-cm baking dish all over with a little butter.

2 ***Arrange the bread cubes*** in a single layer on a rimmed baking sheet and bake until lightly toasted, 8 to 10 minutes. (They will be starting to turn golden around the edges.) Let the bread cubes cool for a few minutes on the sheet and then transfer them to a large bowl.

3 ***In a small saucepan,*** melt the 2 tbsp butter over medium-low heat. After the butter has melted, continue to cook it, swirling the pan occasionally, until the milk solids turn nutty brown. (This can take anywhere from 3 to 6 minutes, depending on the pan you're using.) Remove the pan from the heat and stir in 2 tbsp of the maple syrup. Drizzle the brown butter–maple mixture over the bread cubes, stirring the bread as you drizzle, and toss well. Sprinkle the bread crumbs with a little salt and toss again.

4 ***Fill a wide, large pot two-thirds full of water.*** Add 2 tsp salt and bring to a boil. Add the kale to the boiling water and start timing immediately. Taste a leaf after 4 minutes. It should not be tough or rubbery. If it is, cook for 1 to 2 minutes longer. Drain the kale very thoroughly in a fine-mesh colander in the sink. Rinse with cool water until cool enough to handle. Squeeze handfuls of the kale to remove as much excess liquid as possible and then use your fingers to loosen and separate the kale so that it isn't clumped together.

5 ***In a medium heavy nonstick skillet,*** cook the bacon over medium-low heat until crisp and browned, 10 to 14 minutes. Transfer the bacon to a paper towel–lined plate and let cool. When the bacon is cool enough to handle, break it up into smaller pieces. Pour off half of the bacon fat. Add the scallions to the skillet and cook, stirring, until softened and beginning to brown, about 2 minutes. Add the kale, stir well to coat the kale with the scallions and pan drippings, and remove the pan from the heat.

6 ***In a large mixing bowl,*** whisk together the eggs, milk, cream, remaining 1 tbsp maple syrup, sherry vinegar, several grinds of pepper, and 3/4 tsp salt until well combined.

7 ***Arrange half of the bread cubes*** in a single layer in the prepared baking dish. Top with half of the bacon (including any crumbs), half of the kale and scallion mixture, and one-third of the Parmigiano. Repeat with the remaining bread, bacon, and veggies, and another third of the cheese. Pour the egg mixture evenly over everything. (Start at one end and pour slowly back and forth.) Using your hands, gently press down on the bread and veggies to force the custard to evenly surround everything. Top with the remaining Parmigiano. Let sit for about 20 minutes and gently press down again.

8 ***Bake in the preheated oven*** until the bread pudding has risen and is set and dry in the middle (it will be golden all over), 40 to 45 minutes. Let settle for a few minutes and serve hot or very warm.

Spring Celebration Bread Pudding

with Asparagus, Peas, Shallots, Chives & Fontina

3 tbsp UNSALTED BUTTER, plus more for the baking dish

½ lb/225 g CHALLAH (about ½ loaf), cut into 1-in/2.5-cm cubes

2 tsp HONEY

2 tbsp EXTRA-VIRGIN OLIVE OIL

1 bunch medium ASPARAGUS, trimmed and cut on a sharp diagonal into thin slices (about 2⅓ cups/230 g)

KOSHER SALT

1 cup/115 g thinly sliced SHALLOTS (3 or 4 medium)

8 large EGGS

2 cups/480 ml WHOLE MILK

1 cup/240 ml HEAVY CREAM

1 tsp finely grated LEMON ZEST

1 tsp finely chopped peeled FRESH GINGER

⅛ tsp GROUND NUTMEG

¼ cup/9 g sliced FRESH CHIVES

½ cup/60 g FROZEN PEAS, thawed, or ½ cup/50 g FRESH PEAS, blanched

⅓ cup/40 g coarsely grated PARMIGIANO-REGGIANO (I use the food processor; see page 212.)

4 oz/115 g coarsely grated FONTINA, MONTEREY JACK, or other MILD CREAMY WHITE CHEESE

{Savory Bread Puddings} It's hard to say whether this lovely bread pudding makes a better supper or breakfast, whether it should be brunch or lunch . . . it's just that flexible. It's hearty and light at the same time—plenty filling for the swarthy and plenty elegant for the savvy. You could serve it for Mother's Day or a baby shower, bring it to a potluck, or just throw it together for dinner. Okay, I'll stop; you get the idea. The subtle flavors work together here seamlessly: Just a little lemon and a bit of ginger brighten the custard, while the sautéed shallots and asparagus add earthiness. I like to use a mild, creamy cheese like Fontina in this bread pudding, but a more assertive cheese like Gruyère could also pair well with the asparagus. As with the other bread puddings, there's no need to let the filling sit for longer than 20 minutes before baking, though you can assemble it ahead and refrigerate it for up to 2 hours before putting it in the oven, if you like.

SERVES 6

1 ***Preheat the oven to 375°F/190°C/gas 5.*** Position a rack in the center of the oven. Rub a 13-by-9-in/33-by-23-cm baking dish all over with a little butter.

2 ***Arrange the bread cubes*** in a single layer on a rimmed baking sheet and bake until lightly toasted, 8 to 10 minutes. (They will be starting to turn golden brown around the edges.) Let the bread cubes cool for a few minutes on the sheet and then transfer them to a large bowl.

3 ***In a small saucepan,*** melt 2 tbsp of the butter over medium-low heat. After the butter has melted, continue to cook it, swirling the pan occasionally, until the milk solids turn nutty brown. (This can take anywhere from 3 to 6 minutes, depending on the pan you're using.) Remove the pan from the heat and stir in the honey. Drizzle the brown butter–honey mixture over the bread cubes, stirring as you drizzle and toss well. Set aside.

4 ***In a medium heavy nonstick skillet,*** heat 1 tbsp of the olive oil and 1/2 tbsp of the butter over medium-high heat. When the butter has melted, add the asparagus and 1/4 tsp salt. Cook, stirring, until the asparagus is crisp-tender (it will still be somewhat green), 3 to 4 minutes. Transfer the asparagus to a plate.

5 ***Add the remaining 1 tbsp olive oil*** and 1/2 tbsp butter to the pan and reduce the heat to medium-low. Add the shallots and a pinch of salt and cook, stirring, until the shallots are very soft and lightly golden, 8 to 10 minutes.

6 ***In a large mixing bowl,*** whisk together the eggs, milk, cream, lemon zest, ginger, nutmeg, chives, and 3/4 tsp salt until well combined.

7 ***Arrange half of the bread cubes*** in a single layer in the prepared baking dish. Top with half of the asparagus, half of the shallots, half of the peas, half of the Parmigiano, and half of the Fontina. Repeat with the remaining bread, veggies, and cheese. (Be sure to scrape out any drippings from the bread bowl.) Pour the egg mixture evenly over everything. (Start at one end and pour slowly back and forth.) Using your hands, gently press down on the bread and veggies to force the custard to evenly surround everything. Let sit for 20 minutes, and gently press down again.

8 ***Bake in the preheated oven*** until the bread pudding has risen and is set and dry in the middle (it will be golden all over), 40 to 45 minutes. Let settle for a few minutes and serve hot or very warm.

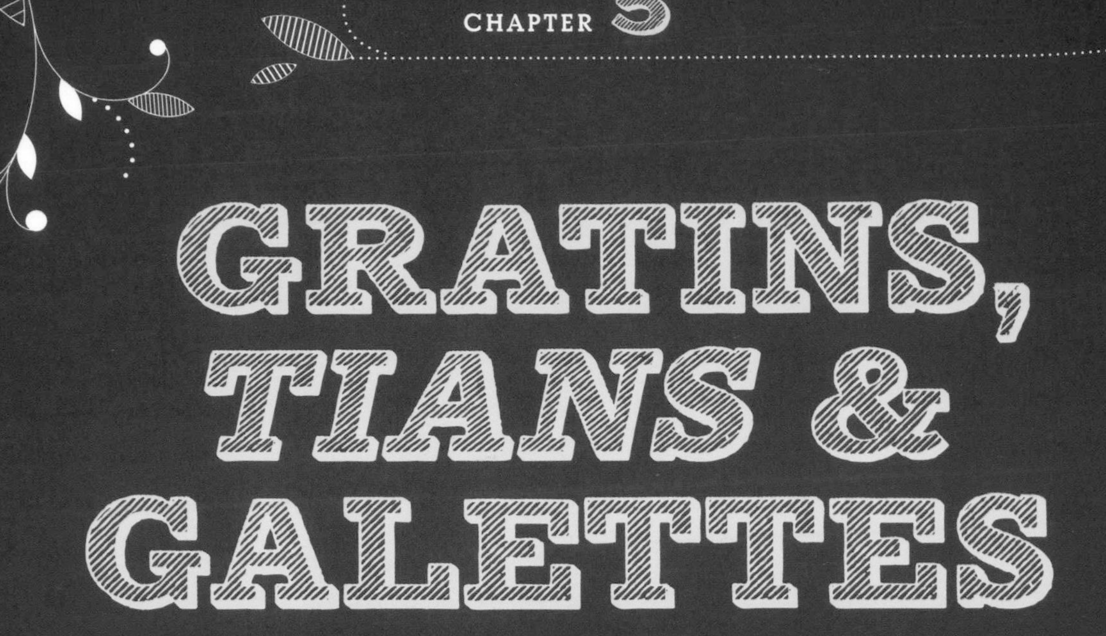

CHAPTER 5

GRATINS, TIANS & GALETTES

Making Gratins, *Tians* & Galettes: How It Works

It's true. I had a Suzy Homemaker oven as a little girl. I thought it was invented for me; I just didn't know why they spelled my name wrong. I loved that tiny turquoise oven that cooked with a light bulb. I made odd-tasting little cakes in it, which my big sister often stole. (Couldn't have been that bad; she has good taste.) But I didn't cook any vegetables in it. A couple of decades went by before my oven obsession—and my love of veggies—kicked in.

These days, there's nothing I won't do with a vegetable and an oven, which is why I had such a hard time narrowing recipes for this (oven-centric) chapter. In the end, channeling my fun-loving Suzy Homemaker self, I went with one style of dish that's the most fun for the cook—and that my sister and other friends happen to love. It's basically a layered vegetable casserole that masquerades as any one of three dishes with fancy names—gratin, *tian*, and galette.

Gratins, cooked in a shallow baking dish until browned and bubbly, are the heartiest (and, yes, the richest) of the bunch. If you're not familiar with a gratin, think of potatoes au gratin (a.k.a. scalloped potatoes), and imagine swapping out some or all the potatoes for other veggies. One of my favorite combinations is sweet potatoes and potatoes (see page 98), which I enhance with an extra layer of flavor (and color) on the bottom—caramelized leeks, spinach, and garlic. Those veggies bake in flavorful liquids until tender, but I also make a style of gratin for which I fully cook the veggies first—by roasting, of course. This bumps up flavor and cuts down on final cooking time. I sometimes make a third style of gratin, too: an elegant showcase for leafy greens, enhanced with a classic white sauce, or béchamel—think creamed spinach but with Swiss chard or another green instead of the spinach.

A *tian* could be defined as a gratin without the cream, but it's more special than that. Originating in the south of France, a *tian* is a lovely showcase for vegetables. Not only do you arrange the veggies in pretty rows (on top of a layer of sautéed aromatic veggies), but you also cook the *tian* long enough for all the veggie juices, herbs, and aromatics to mingle for the most outstanding flavor.

But maybe, just maybe, my favorite way to layer vegetables is in a galette. In the culinary world, a galette can be any number of round, baked creations (often involving pastry). But in my world, a galette is an elegant vegetable pie without a crust. You make one by arranging concentric layers of thinly sliced vegetables (along with just a bit of cheese, olive oil, and herbs) in a tart or springform pan with a removable bottom. After baking, you unmold the tender, golden-brown galette and cut it into wedges. (Serve with a big salad and a bowl of soup for an all-veggie dinner.) After you've tried the potato (my favorite) and eggplant galettes here, experiment with thinly sliced butternut squash, sweet potatoes, and even tomatoes.

Sweet Potato, Spinach & Caramelized-Leek Gratin

with Pecan Crumb Topping

2 tbsp UNSALTED BUTTER, plus more for the baking dish

¾ cup/180 ml HEAVY CREAM

1 cup/70 g FRESH BREAD CRUMBS

⅓ cup/35 g finely chopped TOASTED PECANS (page 198)

2 tbsp EXTRA-VIRGIN OLIVE OIL

2 tsp chopped FRESH PARSLEY, plus 1 tbsp

KOSHER SALT

2 cups thinly sliced LEEKS (white and light green parts from about 2 large leeks, about 6 oz/170 g), thoroughly washed

1 tsp minced GARLIC

4 oz/115 g BABY SPINACH LEAVES (about 4 cups packed)

12 oz/340 g SWEET POTATOES (I like Garnet or Gem varieties.)

8 oz/225 g RUSSET POTATOES

½ cup/40 g coarsely grated SHARP CHEDDAR

1 tsp DIJON MUSTARD

FRESHLY GROUND PEPPER

{Gratins} I love the pretty layers in this gratin and the surprise of the green spinach and leeks peeking out underneath the orange and white potatoes. It's not just the colors, though; those sweet leeks and a bit of garlic deepen the flavor of this gratin, which also gets personality from a little Cheddar cheese and a savory toasted pecan and bread crumb topping. Of course it would make any Thanksgiving table proud, but along with a few slices of your favorite roast (if you're a meatie) or a bowl of Southwestern Spiced Butternut Squash & Apple Soup (page 34) and a few Buttery Popovers (page 205) it could also be dinner for you and some friends on a Saturday night. This takes a bit of time to prep, but once you get it in the oven, you're free to chat with your guests.

SERVES 4

1 ***Preheat the oven to 350°F/180°C/gas 4.*** Rub a shallow 2-qt/2-L gratin or other baking dish with a little butter. Combine the cream with ¾ cup/180 ml water in a liquid measure and set aside.

2 ***In a small bowl,*** combine the bread crumbs, pecans, 1 tbsp of the olive oil, the 2 tsp parsley, and a big pinch of salt. Stir well and set aside.

3 ***In a medium heavy nonstick skillet,*** heat the 2 tbsp butter and the remaining 1 tbsp olive oil over medium-low heat. When the butter has melted, add the leeks and 1/4 tsp salt, cover, and cook, stirring occasionally, until softened and translucent, about 5 minutes. Uncover, raise the heat to medium, and continue to cook, stirring frequently, until the leeks have shrunk and browned in places (some more than others), about 8 minutes more. Add the garlic and stir until softened and fragrant, about 30 seconds. Add all the spinach to the pan and toss with the leeks until the spinach has completely wilted, about 1 minute. Transfer the leeks and spinach to the gratin dish and smooth with a silicone spatula into one thin, even layer.

4 ***Peel the sweet potatoes and potatoes.*** Halve them lengthwise and turn the halves cut-side down. Using a very sharp knife (a santoku is good for this), cut them crosswise into very thin (1/16-in-/2-mm-thick) half-moon slices. (It's more important to get thin rather than perfectly shaped slices.) Put the sweet potatoes and the potatoes in a mixing bowl. Add the cream–water mixture, the cheese, the remaining parsley, the mustard, 3/4 tsp salt, and several grinds of pepper. Mix well.

5 ***Using your hands,*** lift the sweet potatoes and potatoes out of the bowl and transfer them to the prepared dish, arranging them as evenly as possible over the spinach and leeks. Pour and scrape the liquids and anything remaining in the bowl into the dish and distribute everything evenly, adjusting the potatoes and sweet potatoes as necessary to even the top.

6 ***Using your palms,*** press down on the veggies to bring the liquids up and around them as much as possible. (They won't necessarily be completely covered.) Top with an even layer of the bread crumb mixture.

7 ***Bake in the preheated oven*** until the veggies are tender when pierced with a paring knife or fork (check the middle of the dish as well as the sides), the bread crumbs are brown, and the juices around the edges of the gratin have bubbled down and formed a dark brown rim around the edge, 60 to 65 minutes. Let cool for 15 minutes before serving.

Roasted Cauliflower, Potato, Mushroom & Green Bean Gratin

with Shallots, Gruyère & Rosemary

¼ cup/60 ml plus 2 tsp EXTRA-VIRGIN OLIVE OIL, plus more for the baking dish

¾ cup/50 g coarse FRESH BREAD CRUMBS (I like English muffins for these; see page 212.)

1½ tsp chopped FRESH ROSEMARY

KOSHER SALT

12 oz/340 g CAULIFLOWER FLORETS, each about 1½ in/4 cm long and 1 in/2.5 cm wide and cut with one flat side

12 oz/340 g YUKON GOLD POTATOES, unpeeled, cut into small (about ⅜-in-/1-cm-square) dice

6 oz/170 g GREEN BEANS, trimmed and cut into 1-in-/2.5-cm-long pieces

6 oz/170 g medium CREMINI MUSHROOMS, quartered

4 to 5 small SHALLOTS (4 oz/115 g), quartered and peeled (if you can only find large shallots, you will need only 2 to 3 cut lengthwise into several pieces)

¾ cup/60 g grated GRUYÈRE

¾ cup/180 ml HEAVY CREAM

{Gratins} Oh my, I do love this gratin. These vegetables are so made for each other, and when they're all roasted, their flavors get even more intense and more in sync with each other. Add nutty Gruyère cheese and rosemary, and you have one flavorful dish. This gratin is more loosely jumbled than the Sweet Potato, Spinach & Caramelized-Leek Gratin (page 98), because the vegetables are already cooked and therefore there's no need to cram them tightly in the pan and completely cover them with liquid. All you have to do is toss the cooked veggies into the pan, scatter on the cheese, add the cream, and top with bread crumbs. Just a short time in the oven, and the whole thing will be golden and crusty. This richly flavored gratin calls out for a big hearty green salad alongside it. The Winter Green & White Side Salad (page 195) would be perfect.

SERVES 3

1 ***Preheat the oven to 475°F/240°C/gas 9.*** Line two large heavy-duty rimmed baking sheets with parchment. Rub a shallow 2-qt/2-L gratin or baking dish with olive oil.

2 ***In a small bowl,*** combine the bread crumbs, 1 tsp of the olive oil, ½ tsp of the rosemary, and a pinch of salt. Mix well and set aside.

3 ***In a mixing bowl,*** toss the cauliflower, potatoes, green beans, mushrooms, and shallots with the ¼ cup/60 ml olive oil and 1 tsp salt. Divide the vegetables evenly between the two prepared baking sheets and arrange in a single layer. Roast, rotating the sheets from front to back and between upper and lower oven racks halfway through cooking, until the potatoes are tender and the other veggies have browned in places, 24 to 28 minutes. Let the veggies cool for 10 minutes on the baking sheets. When cool, transfer all the veggies to the prepared baking dish. (The outer layer of some of the shallots may get overly crisp when roasted; just remove these before transferring the veggies to the baking dish.)

4 ***Reduce the oven temperature*** to 425°F/220°C/gas 7.

5 ***Top the vegetables*** with the remaining rosemary and the cheese and toss them gently with your fingers to incorporate the cheese a bit. Drizzle the cream over the vegetables. Top with the bread crumb mixture, leaving some vegetables peeking out.

6 ***Bake in the preheated oven*** until the bread crumbs are well browned and the cream is bubbly and reduced, leaving a thin brown ring around the edge, 18 to 20 minutes. Serve hot or warm.

Individual Swiss Chard Gratins

with Garlic Cream

1½ tbsp UNSALTED BUTTER, plus more for greasing the dishes

⅔ cup/45 g FRESH BREAD CRUMBS (I like English muffins for these; see page 212.)

⅓ cup/40 g plus 1 tbsp coarsely grated PARMIGIANO-REGGIANO

1 tbsp chopped FRESH PARSLEY (optional)

1 tbsp EXTRA-VIRGIN OLIVE OIL, plus more if needed

KOSHER SALT

2¾ lb/1.3 kg (about 3 bunches) SWISS CHARD (I like Bright Lights or Rainbow variety), washed and stemmed

4 large GARLIC CLOVES, well smashed and peeled

¾ cup/180 ml WHOLE MILK

½ cup/120 ml HEAVY CREAM

1½ tbsp ALL-PURPOSE FLOUR

⅛ tsp BALSAMIC VINEGAR

FRESHLY GROUND PEPPER

{Gratins} Everybody loves a mini, and a mini gratin is no exception. This one is a silky version of classic creamed spinach—with Swiss chard standing in for the spinach. The "silky" part comes from a simple white sauce (infused with a little garlic) that you make on the stovetop. Once you've mixed in the chard, filled your custard cups, and topped them with Parmigiano crumbs, the gratins need only about 25 minutes in the oven. If you don't have custard cups, ramekins, or other ovenproof baking dishes that measure 8 to 10 oz/240 to 300 ml, most grocery stores have 10-oz/300-ml heatproof glass custard cups. You could also use two 2-cup/480-ml baking dishes or one 4-cup/960-ml baking dish. There's a generous amount of white sauce here, so if your three bunches of chard yield just a bit more than 1 lb/455 g of leaves, go ahead and use them. This would make an elegant vegetarian main dish for a special dinner, like Valentine's Day. Start the meal with Roasted Beet & Shallot Salad with Mint & Sopressata Crisps (page 26), and serve Buttery Popovers (page 205), too.

SERVES 4

1 ***Preheat the oven to 375°F/190°C/gas 5.*** Position a rack in the upper third of the oven. Rub a little butter all over the inside of four 8- to 10-oz/240- to 300-ml custard cups or other 1-cup/240-ml ovenproof baking dishes. For easier baking, put the dishes on a small, rimmed heavy-duty baking sheet.

2 ***In a small bowl,*** combine the bread crumbs, 1 tbsp of the Parmigiano, the parsley (if using), 1 tsp of the olive oil, and a pinch of salt. Mix well and set aside.

3 ***Put a large colander in your sink*** or over a bowl. In a large nonstick skillet, heat 1 tsp of the olive oil over medium heat. Add half of the Swiss chard and ¼ tsp salt. Let the chard sit for 1 minute, then begin flipping it with tongs, moving the wilted chard from the bottom to the top of the raw chard so that all the leaves get some contact with the pan. Stir and flip until all the leaves have wilted, about 2 minutes. Transfer the chard to the colander and repeat with the remaining chard, adding 1 tsp of the olive oil and another ¼ tsp salt.

⟶

4 ***Let all the chard drain*** and cool in the colander for several minutes. When cool, transfer it to a cutting board, spread it out, and chop it coarsely. (Smaller pieces of chard are nicer in the finished gratin, but it's totally up to you how much you want to chop it.) Leave the chopped chard on the cutting board until you need it. It will continue to steam off a bit of moisture.

5 ***In a medium saucepan,*** combine the garlic, milk, and cream and bring to a boil. (Watch the liquids carefully so that they do not boil over.) Immediately remove the pan from the heat and let sit for 10 minutes to allow the garlic to infuse the cream. While the cream is sitting, stir it occasionally with a silicone spatula to prevent a skin from forming.

6 ***In another medium saucepan (nonstick works well),*** melt the 1½ tbsp butter over medium-low heat. Add the flour and whisk until well blended. (Either a flat whisk or a small silicone whisk will work best here. Be sure to whisk in the seam of the pan.) Cook, stirring constantly, for 1 minute. Remove the pan from the heat.

7 ***With a fork,*** remove most of the smashed garlic from the milk-cream mixture, pushing the pieces against the side of the pot to squeeze out all the flavorful liquid. (Don't worry if any small pieces remain in the liquid.) Season the liquid with ½ tsp salt, the balsamic vinegar, and a few grinds of pepper. Stir well.

8 ***Return the pan with the flour-butter mixture*** to medium-low heat and add the milk-cream mixture to it in a slow, steady stream, whisking constantly. Raise the heat to medium and continue to whisk constantly. The sauce will begin to thicken up. As soon as bubbles start appearing, whisk constantly for just about 1 minute more and then remove the pan from the heat. The sauce should have a velvety smooth texture and be thick enough to coat the back of a spoon but still fall off the whisk in a stream.

9 ***Transfer the chopped chard*** to a large heatproof (stainless-steel) mixing bowl. Pour and scrape all the cream sauce over the chard and mix thoroughly. Add the remaining ⅓ cup/40 g Parmigiano and stir to incorporate. Divide the creamy chard mixture evenly among the 4 prepared cups and top each with the bread-crumb mixture.

10 ***Bake in the preheated oven*** until the bread crumbs are lightly browned and the mixture is bubbling, 18 minutes. Let sit for a couple minutes and serve warm.

Mediterranean Zucchini, Tomato & Bell Pepper *Tian*

with Pine-Nut Crumb Topping

{Tians} It wouldn't be possible for me to write a main-dish vegetable cookbook without including one of my layered summer vegetable dishes. Over the years, I've done lots of variations on these Provençal *tians*, and my friends tell me they make them over and over again. The secret to their flavor is letting them cook long enough for the tomato (and other vegetable) juices to reduce, caramelize, and mingle with the onions. But this particular recipe gets added flavor from sun-dried tomatoes and bell peppers on the bottom, and pine nuts in the top crust. I love to cook it in my enameled cast-iron oval gratin dish, but other 2-qt/2-L shallow baking dishes, like a 9-by-7-in/23-by-17-cm heatproof glass one, work fine, too. Take this dish to a potluck or picnic. It will be a hit, I promise. But if by chance you wind up with any leftovers, you'll love those, too, as it tastes great the next day.

SERVES 4

⟶

2 tsp EXTRA-VIRGIN OLIVE OIL, plus 5 tbsp/75 ml and more for the baking dish

3 tbsp chopped TOASTED PINE NUTS (see page 198)

¾ cup/115 g cup FRESH BREAD CRUMBS

¾ cup/85 g coarsely grated PARMIGIANO-REGGIANO (I use the food processor; see p. 212.)

1 tbsp chopped FRESH THYME

2 tsp BALSAMIC VINEGAR

2 tsp HONEY

KOSHER SALT

1½ small ZUCCHINI (about 12 oz/340 g), cut on the diagonal into thin (⅛- to 3⁄16-in-/3- to 5-mm-thick) slices

1¼ lb/570 g (about 4 or 5) small to medium red and orange ripe TOMATOES, cored and cut into 3⁄16 -in-/5-mm-thick slices (If using medium tomatoes, halve them before slicing.)

2 small ONIONS, cut crosswise into thin slices (about 1¾ cups)

1 small or ½ large RED or YELLOW BELL PEPPER (about 4 oz/115 g), cored and very thinly sliced

2 tsp minced GARLIC

3 tbsp finely chopped OIL-PACKED SUN-DRIED TOMATOES, drained

1 ***Preheat the oven to 375°F/190°/gas 5.*** Rub a shallow 2-qt/2-L baking dish with a little olive oil. In a small bowl, combine the pine nuts, bread crumbs, 2 tbsp of the Parmigiano, ½ tsp of the thyme, and the 2 tsp olive oil. Mix well.

2 ***In a small bowl,*** whisk together the vinegar, honey, 2 tbsp of the olive oil, and ¼ tsp salt. Put the zucchini slices in one medium bowl and the tomato slices in another. Add a pinch of salt and 1 tsp thyme to each bowl, and drizzle each with half of the vinegar mixture. Toss gently. Let sit while you prepare the rest of the recipe.

3 ***In a medium heavy nonstick skillet,*** heat 1 tbsp of the olive oil over medium heat. Add the onions, bell pepper, and ¼ tsp salt. Cook, stirring frequently, until the onions and bell pepper are limp and the onions are golden brown, 10 to 12 minutes. Stir in the garlic and cook until softened and fragrant, about 30 seconds. Transfer the onions and bell pepper to the prepared baking dish and spread them in an even layer. Let cool slightly. Top the veggies with the sun-dried tomatoes and the remaining ½ tsp thyme.

4 ***Starting at a narrow end of the baking dish,*** arrange a row of overlapping tomato slices across the dish, propping the slices up against the end of the dish at an angle as you go. Sprinkle a little Parmigiano on the row of tomatoes and then arrange a row of zucchini slices, slightly overlapping each other and slightly overlapping the row of tomatoes. Sprinkle Parmigiano on that row and continue to arrange alternating rows of tomatoes and zucchini, sprinkling each with Parmigiano, until you get to the other end of the dish. You should have just about the right amount of zucchini, but don't worry if you have extra slices; you will definitely have extra tomato slices (and ones that you've chosen not to use because they've fallen apart!). But as you are going along, if it looks like you will have a lot of extras, gently push the rows back up toward the end of the dish where you started to make room for a few more rows.

5 ***Scrape any remaining seasoning*** and juices from the bowl with the zucchini over the veggies. (Leave the extra tomato juices behind or use them in a gazpacho!) Sprinkle any remaining Parmigiano over the veggies. Drizzle the veggies with the remaining 2 tbsp olive oil and top with the bread crumb–pine nut mixture.

6 ***Bake in the preheated oven*** until well browned and the juices have bubbled for a while and considerably reduced, about 65 minutes. Let cool at least 15 minutes before serving.

Butternut Squash, Jonagold Apple & Caramelized Onion *Tian*

5 tbsp/70 g **UNSALTED BUTTER**, plus more for the baking dish

1 cup/70 g **FRESH BREAD CRUMBS** made from English muffins (see page 212)

1 tbsp mixed coarsely chopped **FRESH SAGE, ROSEMARY,** and **THYME**

1 tbsp **EXTRA-VIRGIN OLIVE OIL**

2 medium or 3 small **ONIONS**, thinly sliced (about 2 cups)

KOSHER SALT

12 oz/340 g peeled **BUTTERNUT SQUASH**, neck only (One 10- or 11-oz/280- or 310-g piece will usually provide enough slices.)

1½ large **JONAGOLD APPLES** (7 to 8 oz/200 to 225 g each)

⅓ cup/75 ml **APPLE CIDER**

1 tsp **HONEY**

{Tians} This is an elegant *tian* with no cream or cheese in it, just pure intense flavor from the likes of apple cider, caramelized onions, a little brown butter, and one of my favorite apples, Jonagold. Arranging the pretty rows of thinly sliced squash and apples in this *tian*-style gratin will satisfy the artist in you, too. I included Jonagold in the name of this dish to encourage you to use a complexly flavored apple; you can choose another baking apple, but they vary a lot in flavor. One of my testers used the tangy, firm Pink Lady with great results. And while this is special enough to be a main attraction, a small portion goes a long way, so plan to serve this with a little meat or with another green veggie, like the Green Bean, Red Onion & Cherry Tomato Ragoût with Pomegranate Pan Sauce (page 138). I like to use my enameled cast-iron gratin pan for this, as it promotes more caramelization (see Sources, page 216). If you use heatproof glass or ceramic, just add a few more minutes to the baking time for the same doneness.

SERVES 4

1 ***Preheat the oven to 375°F/190°/gas 5.*** Rub a shallow 2-qt/2-L baking dish with a little butter. Melt 1 tbsp of the butter in the microwave or in a small skillet over low heat. In a small bowl, combine the melted butter, bread crumbs, and 1/2 tsp of the mixed fresh herbs. Use your fingers to mix thoroughly and moisten the crumbs.

2 ***In a medium heavy nonstick skillet,*** heat 1 tbsp of the butter and the olive oil over medium-low heat. Add the onions and 1/4 tsp salt and stir well. Cover and cook, stirring occasionally, until the onions are softened and translucent, 6 to 7 minutes. Uncover, raise the heat to medium, and cook, stirring frequently, until the onions are golden brown, 7 to 8 minutes more. Remove the pan from the heat and let the onions cool for a few minutes. Transfer the onions to the prepared baking dish and spread them in an even layer.

3 ***Quarter the squash neck lengthwise.*** (Or if you buy the squash peeled, it will already be halved, so just halve those pieces lengthwise.) Cut the long pieces crosswise into thin (about 1/8-in-/3-mm-thick) slices. Peel, quarter, and cut the core from the apples. Cut the quarters crosswise into thin (about 1/8-in-/3-mm-thick) slices.

4 ***Starting at a narrow end of the baking dish,*** arrange a row of overlapping squash slices across the dish, propping the slices up against the end of the dish at an angle as you go. Season the squash with a tiny bit of salt and a sprinkling of the fresh herbs. Next, arrange a row of overlapping apple slices. (You will have to stand them up a bit and lean them against the row of squash.) Season the apples with a tiny bit of salt and a sprinkling of the fresh herbs. Continue arranging alternating rows of squash and apples, seasoning as you go, until the pan is full or until you have used up most of your slices. (You may have to gently push back the rows in order to fit in a few more rows.) Sprinkle any remaining herbs over the whole *tian*.

5 ***In a small saucepan,*** melt the remaining 3 tbsp butter over medium-low heat. After the butter has melted, continue to cook it, swirling the pan occasionally, until the milk solids turn nutty brown. (This can take anywhere from 3 to 6 minutes.) Remove the pan from the heat and stir in the apple cider and honey. Use a silicone spatula or wooden spoon to scrape up any browned milk solids that have stuck to the bottom of the pan.

6 ***Drizzle the butter-cider-honey mixture*** over the *tian*, taking care to cover as much area as possible. Top the *tian* with the bread crumb mixture.

7 ***Bake in the preheated oven*** until the top is golden brown (there will be a brown ring around the edge of the dish) and the squash and apples are very tender, 50 to 55 minutes. (Cooking time will be 5 to 10 minutes longer in a heatproof glass baking dish than in an enameled cast-iron dish.) Let sit for just a few minutes (the *tian* will absorb some of the juices in the pan), and serve warm.

Potato Galette

with Rosemary & Two Cheeses

{Galettes} This is one of my very favorite potato creations, a much easier version of a fancy French dish called potatoes Anna, which you cook and flip in a skillet. No flipping here. You make the galette in a tart pan or springform pan with a removable bottom, and the layers of thinly sliced potatoes and tasty cheeses bake down into a crispy potato pie that's tender on the inside, golden brown on the outside. It's fun to assemble, lovely to look at, tasty to eat, and it reheats well, too. I've made potato (and sweet potato) galettes with different herbs and cheeses, but this recipe features my favorite combination: Yukon gold potatoes, rosemary, Gruyère, and Parmigiano. For an all-veggie dinner, serve a wedge of this with a salad and Asparagus & Leek Bisque with Crème Fraîche & Tarragon (page 38). Make this same meal for fish lovers, but top the wedge of galette with a small piece of sear-roasted salmon.

SERVES 4

→

½ tsp EXTRA-VIRGIN OLIVE OIL, plus 3½ tbsp and more for drizzling

1¾ lb/800 g YUKON GOLD POTATOES (about 6 medium-small), unpeeled

1¼ tsp chopped FRESH ROSEMARY

½ cup/55 g finely grated PARMIGIANO-REGGIANO plus 2 tbsp

¾ cup/60 g grated GRUYÈRE

KOSHER SALT

1 ***Preheat the oven to 375°F/190°C/gas 5.*** Position a rack in the center of the oven. Brush a 9-in/23-cm tart pan or a 9½-in/24-cm springform pan with the ½ tsp olive oil. (Make sure the pan has a removable bottom.) Put the pan on a parchment-lined rimmed baking sheet.

2 ***Put the potatoes on your cutting board*** and trim a small slice from the bottom of each potato to stabilize it. Trim off and discard the very ends of the potatoes. Then cut the potatoes crosswise into very thin (between 1/16 and 1/8 in/2 and 3 mm thick; they should bend easily) slices. A *santoku* knife works great for this. You don't need a mandoline or paper-thin slices; just aim to cut slices as thinly as you comfortably can.

3 ***Put the potato slices,*** 1 tsp of the rosemary, and the 3½ tbsp olive oil in a mixing bowl and toss thoroughly to coat.

4 ***Divide the ½ cup/55 g Parmigiano into thirds.*** Divide the Gruyère into thirds.

5 ***Cover the bottom of the tart pan*** with a layer of potato slices, starting by making a ring of slightly overlapping slices all the way around the outside edge and then working inward, laying down more rings of slightly overlapping slices until the bottom is covered. Sprinkle the potatoes with a tiny bit of salt (about 1/8 tsp) and then top with a third of the Gruyère and a third of the Parmigiano. Arrange another layer of potatoes over that, season again with salt, top again with a third of each of the cheeses, and repeat with a third layer of potatoes, salt, and cheeses. Finish with a top (fourth) layer of potatoes. Discard any extra potato slices. (If you are using a tart pan, it will look very full. Don't worry; the potatoes will cook down.) Drizzle the potatoes with a little olive oil and sprinkle them with a little salt, the remaining ¼ tsp rosemary, and the 2 tbsp Parmigiano.

6 ***Bake in the preheated oven*** until the top is golden brown and a fork easily pierces the layers of potato, 55 to 60 minutes. Let the galette cool for 10 minutes in the pan. Run a paring knife around the inside edge, if necessary, and remove the outer ring of the pan. Slide a thin spatula under the galette all the way around to loosen it and, holding it at an angle, gently slide it off onto a cutting board. Cut into quarters and serve. You can also refrigerate the wedges at this point and reheat them in a moderate oven for 10 to 15 minutes.

Roasted Eggplant Galette

with Mint, Honey & Lemony Arugula Salad

5 tbsp/75 ml EXTRA-VIRGIN OLIVE OIL, plus 2 tsp and more for the pan

1 tbsp ORANGE JUICE

1 tsp BALSAMIC VINEGAR

1 tsp minced GARLIC

1/2 tsp LEMON ZEST

1¼ lb/570 g GLOBE EGGPLANT, ends trimmed, skin peeled, halved, and sliced 1/8 in/3 mm thick

1/2 tsp KOSHER SALT

2 tbsp finely sliced FRESH MINT

¼ cup/20 g coarsely grated PARMIGIANO-REGGIANO

HONEY for drizzling

SIMPLE LEMONY ARUGULA SALAD (page 197)

LEMON WEDGES for serving

GRILLED BREAD (page 203), TOASTED PITA, or WARMED NAAN for serving

If your vegetable garden overflows with eggplants like ours did last fall, you'll love this new and different way to cook and present them. The layers of eggplant in this galette roast slowly and benefit from the moisture they share with each other, developing a deep and silky texture. The finished galette is an impressive rosette that looks lovely with a few greens on top.

SERVES 4 OR 5

1 ***Preheat the oven to 375°/190°C/gas 5.*** Position a rack in the center of the oven. Brush a 9-in/23-cm tart pan or a 9½-in/24-cm springform pan with a little olive oil. (Make sure the pan has a removable bottom.) Put the pan on a parchment-lined rimmed baking sheet.

2 ***In a small bowl,*** combine the 5 tbsp/75 ml olive oil, orange juice, vinegar, garlic, and lemon zest and whisk lightly. Put the eggplant slices in a bowl, sprinkle them with salt and mint, and toss. Drizzle and scrape the olive oil mixture over the eggplant, tossing as you drizzle. Try to distribute the ingredients as even as possible, but don't worry when some of the eggplant slices soak up more of the oil than others. Also, don't worry if a few of the slices break apart while you're tossing.

3 ***Cover the bottom of the tart pan*** with a layer of eggplant slices, starting by making a ring of slightly overlapping slices all the way around the outside edge and then working inward, laying down more rings of slightly overlapping slices until the bottom is completely covered. Sprinkle the eggplant with 1 tbsp of the Parmigiano. Arrange another layer of eggplant slices over that, and sprinkle again with another 1 tbsp of the Parmigiano. Repeat with a third and final layer of eggplant, and drizzle with the remaining 2 tsp olive oil. Scrape any of the herb and oil mixture remaining in the bowl over the galette and top with the remaining 2 tbsp Parmigiano.

4 ***Bake in the preheated oven*** until the top is golden brown, the eggplant slices are tender all the way through, and the galette has shrunk quite a bit, about 1 hour. Let the galette cool for 10 minutes in the pan. Run a paring knife around the inside edge, if necessary, and remove the outer ring of the pan. Slide a thin spatula under the galette all the way around to loosen it and, holding it an angle, gently slide it off onto a cutting board. Cut into four or five wedges and drizzle sparingly with honey. Garnish with the salad and lemon wedges and serve with warm bread.

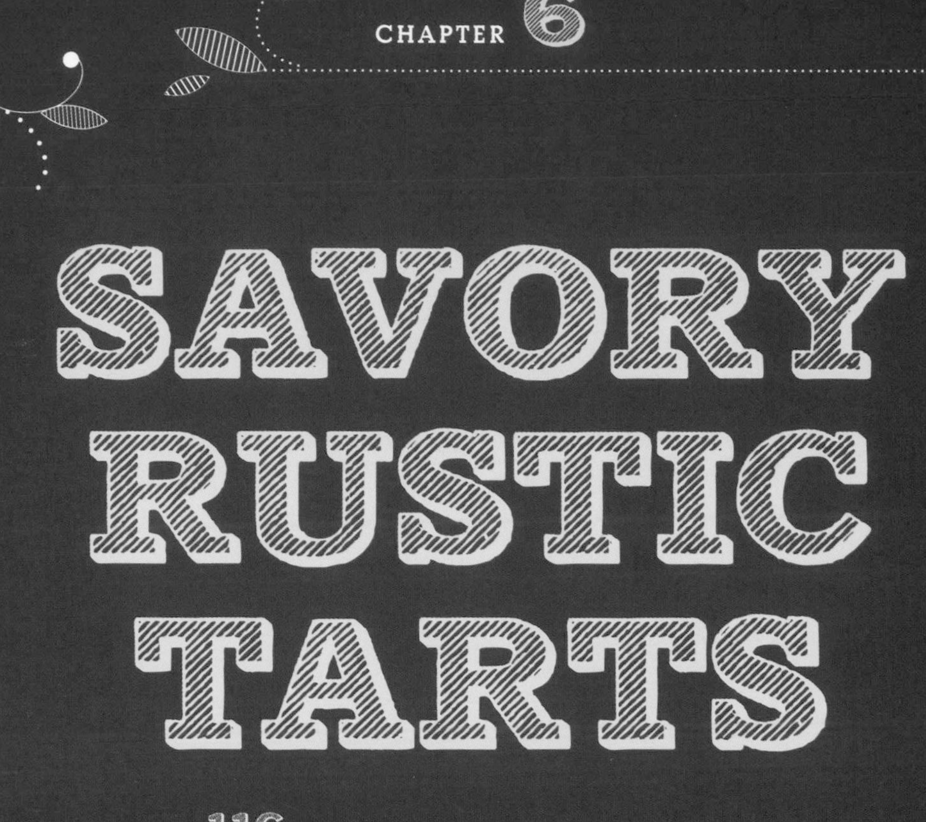
CHAPTER 6
SAVORY
RUSTIC
TARTS

Making a Savory Rustic Tart: How It Works

Used to be, the pastry whizzes were off in one corner, and the rest of us were all off in another. We didn't dare spar with those cool-handed, deft-fingered dough handlers lest we embarrass ourselves silly. Making a good piecrust, much less a flaky tart dough, seemed, well, like a dream. Then along came the food processor and leveled the playing field. If you weren't around the day this annoucement was made, listen up: You can make an amazingly flaky, tender, buttery tart crust without taking a sixteen-week cooking course. And since you'll be filling it with vegetables, you can feel virtuous, too. Okay, I'm kidding about that part.

As much as I absolutely adore these savory tarts, no, you can't eat one every night or sit down and eat a whole one yourself. You won't need to, though; a slice or two of Savoy Cabbage, Apple, Onion & Gruyère Rustic Tart tucked into a serving of Winter Green & White Side Salad with Blue Cheese & Hazelnuts (page 195) is so satisfying that you might even skip that cup of Zesty Tomato-Ginger Bisque (page 36).

But before I go on about how delicious these tarts are, how fun they are to make (my kitchen mantra, I know), how they're the absolute best antidote to the cold and dreary doldrums, how there's nary a vegetable that doesn't sing in one of these . . . let me tell you exactly what a savory rustic tart is: It's a free-form, hand-shaped tart. You roll the dough out into a circle, transfer it to a heavy baking sheet, pile the filling in the middle of the dough, and fold the dough up around it in a series of easy pleats. The tart goes into a hot oven, where the cold butter in the dough releases steam as it melts, creating the air pockets that are the secret to an incredibly flaky crust.

My dough, as I mentioned, comes together quickly in a food processor. I don't even suggest another method, since the food processor's blades do an incomparable job of cutting the butter into the flour. I know food processors are expensive, though, so here are two thoughts if you don't have one: Borrow one from a friend! (People are happier than you'd think to be asked, and this way you can give one a test spin.) Second, check online sources for refurbished models, which can be half the price of a new one.

The dough needs to rest in the refrigerator after it's made, so it's best to make it in advance (even a day or two ahead). When it comes out of the fridge, it will need some warm-up time, so you can make your filling then. You can also cook your tart ahead, slice it, and rewarm it gently for serving. If you've got a rolling pin (I like the French tapered kind), a heavy sheet pan, some parchment paper, and (ideally!) a scale to weigh your flour, that's all you'll need. Oh, and a good appetite.

Savory Rustic Tart Dough

2 cups/255 g UNBLEACHED ALL-PURPOSE FLOUR, plus more for dusting

½ tsp TABLE SALT

1 cup/225 g very cold UNSALTED BUTTER, cut into ½-in/12-mm cubes

¼ cup/60 ml ICE WATER

Easy, make-ahead, absolutely delicious—I swear, you no longer have to be afraid of pastry dough; of making it, rolling it out, shaping it, any of that. Yes, you'll need a food processor (my favorite tool for making pizza dough, see page 164, too), but oh, will you be happy with this ultra-buttery flaky crust.

The one thing to keep in mind when making this dough is timing. Making the dough ahead is the best idea. While it only takes 10 minutes to make, the dough needs to rest and chill in the fridge for at least 1 hour, and then, after you take the dough out of the fridge, it will need to warm back up to "cool" room temperature, which will take 45 to 55 minutes. So make the dough some morning or evening when you have a few spare minutes. Shape it into a disk, wrap it up, and pop it into the fridge. Then when you're ready to make a tart, you'll only need to set aside the time it takes to make your filling (and warm the dough back up at the same time). The dough will keep in the fridge for 2 to 3 days and in the freezer for 3 to 4 weeks.

MAKES ENOUGH DOUGH FOR TWO 8- TO 9-IN/20- TO 23-CM TARTS

1 ***In the bowl of a food processor,*** combine the flour and salt. Pulse briefly to combine. Add the butter. Pulse quickly about twenty times, or until the butter particles are quite small (like tiny pebbles). With the motor running, add the ice water in a steady stream. (This will take about 10 seconds.) Stop the motor. Then pulse quickly six or eight times, just until the mixture begins to leave the sides of the bowl and clump together. The mixture will still be somewhat loose and crumbly. That's okay; you will bring the dough together in the next step.

2 ***Turn the mixture out*** into a big mixing bowl and knead it briefly against the sides of the bowl to finish bringing it together as a dough. Once you have incorporated all the crumbs, knead once or twice to smooth it out just a bit. While you don't want to overhandle the dough, you also don't want to be afraid to handle it as much as you need to in order to bring all the bits of the dough together, as it will ultimately be easier to roll out.

3 ***Divide the dough in half.*** (If you have a scale, you can weigh the dough pieces to make sure they're of equal or close-to-equal weight. They should each weigh about 9½ oz/270 g).

4 ***Shape each piece into a disk*** about 1 in/2.5 cm thick (and about 4 in/10 cm across). (Again, don't be afraid to handle the disk just enough to smooth out cracks and make a tidy disk.) Dust lightly with flour, wrap in plastic wrap, and refrigerate for at least 1 hour or up to 2 days. (You will need to remove the dough from the fridge 45 minutes before rolling it.*) Alternatively, you can freeze the dough for up to a month. Thaw it in the fridge overnight before using.

*Depending on how long your dough disk has been refrigerated, it will most likely be between 42° and 50°F/5.5° and 10°C when you take it out. Anything in this range is rock hard. You're looking for the dough to warm up to about 60°F/15.5°C. Don't worry. You don't have to take its temperature; it will be ready when it is still slightly cool but somewhat pliable. Again, depending on the temperature of the chilled dough and the temperature of your kitchen, this will take anywhere from 40 to 60 minutes. Leaving 45 minutes or so is a good bet, but don't worry if you get behind. There is a decent window of time, and on all but the hottest of days (or kitchens), it can usually sit for up to 30 minutes more before it gets too warm.

Savoy Cabbage, Apple, Onion & Gruyère Rustic Tart

FOR THE EGG WASH
1 EGG YOLK

2 tbsp HEAVY CREAM

FOR THE FILLING
1 tbsp EXTRA-VIRGIN OLIVE OIL

2 tbsp UNSALTED BUTTER

1 medium ONION (6 to 7 oz/170 to 200 g), cut crosswise into thin slices

KOSHER SALT

6 oz/170 g SAVOY CABBAGE, thinly sliced (about 3 cups packed)

1/2 GOLDEN DELICIOUS APPLE, unpeeled, cored, and cut into thin (about 1/8-in/3-mm-thick) slices

FOR THE TART
1 cup/85 g grated GRUYÈRE

1 tsp lightly chopped FRESH THYME

FLOUR for dusting

1 disk SAVORY RUSTIC TART DOUGH (page 116)

This tart is a great way to introduce people to this ethereal (and traditionally Alsatian) combination of ingredients. I cook the cabbage high and dry so that it browns (almost toasts) before it steams. This is the secret to bringing out the complex nutty flavor in cabbage. For a nice fall supper with veggie-loving friends, serve a slice of this tart along with the Winter Green & White Side Salad with Blue Cheese and Hazelnuts (page 195) and a bowl of Creamy Double-Mushroom Soup (page 32).

SERVES 4

1 ***Preheat the oven to 400°F/200°C/gas 6.*** Position a rack in the center of the oven.

2 ***To make the egg wash:*** In a small bowl, whisk together the egg yolk and cream, cover with plastic wrap, and set aside.

3 ***To make the filling:*** In a medium heavy nonstick skillet, heat the olive oil and 1 tbsp of the butter over medium-low heat. Add the onion and a pinch of salt, cover, and cook, stirring occasionally, until the onion is limp and translucent, 5 minutes. Uncover, raise the heat to medium, and cook, stirring occasionally, until the onion is golden brown, another 6 to 8 minutes. Transfer the onion to a plate to cool.

4 ***Add 1/2 tbsp of the butter to the pan,*** raise the heat to medium-high, and add the cabbage and a big pinch of salt. Cook, tossing with tongs occasionally (only once or twice at first to let the cabbage have contact with the pan), until the cabbage is limp and nicely browned in spots all over, about 5 minutes. Transfer the cabbage to a separate plate to cool.

5 ***Remove the pan from the heat*** and let it cool for 1 or 2 minutes before returning it to medium heat. And add the remaining 1/2 tbsp butter. When the butter has melted, add the apple slices, season them with a pinch of salt, and spread them out in a single layer. Let them cook undisturbed until very lightly brown on the bottom side, about 2 minutes. Flip and cook them until the other side is lightly browned, another 2 minutes. Transfer the apples to a separate plate to cool.

6 ***To make the tart:*** Line a large heavy-duty rimmed baking sheet with parchment and position it and the cabbage, onion, apple, Gruyère, and thyme around your work surface.

7 ***Sprinkle your work surface*** with flour and spread it around with your hand. Put the disk of dough in front of you and lightly tap it with the rolling pin to start spreading it. Gently roll it out, lifting and giving the disk a quarter-turn after each roll, until you have a roughly 12-in/30.5-cm round. Try not to roll your pin over the edges of the dough, as that will tend to make the edges thinner than the center. (If your edges get ragged or torn, patch them back together or trim them.) If the dough is sticking, lift it up and toss a bit of flour underneath and/or over it. Roll up or drape the dough over your rolling pin, and unroll or undrape it onto the prepared baking sheet.

8 ***Sprinkle 1/4 cup/21 g of the Gruyère*** over the dough, leaving a 2-in/5-cm border around the edge, top with half of the cabbage, then with half of the onion. Sprinkle with a little bit of the thyme and top with another 1/4 cup/21 g of the Gruyère. Repeat with the remaining cabbage and onion, and sprinkle again with a little thyme and another 1/4 cup/21 g of the Gruyère. Arrange the apple, very slightly overlapping, in the center of the tart. (It will not completely cover the filling.) Sprinkle with a bit of thyme and the remaining 1/4 cup/21 g Gruyère.

9 ***Pleat and fold the edges of the dough*** up and over the outer edge of the filling all the way around the tart, about every 2 to 3 in/5 to 7.5 cm. (You will be folding in that 2-in/5-cm border.)

10 ***Brush the edges of the dough*** with the egg wash (you won't use it all), and sprinkle the edges of the tart with any remaining thyme.

11 ***Bake until nicely golden*** all over and crisp and brown on the bottom (check with a spatula), 38 to 40 minutes. Let cool for a few minutes and use the parchment to slide the tart onto a cutting board. Let cool for another 5 to 10 minutes before slicing and serving.

Roasted Butternut Squash, Cranberry, Shallot & Pecan Tart

FOR THE EGG WASH
1 EGG YOLK

2 tbsp HEAVY CREAM

FOR THE FILLING
1 lb/455 g peeled BUTTERNUT SQUASH, cut into 3/8- to 1/2-in/1-cm- to 12-mm dice (about 3½ cups)

2 tbsp EXTRA-VIRGIN OLIVE OIL

KOSHER SALT

1½ tbsp UNSALTED BUTTER

2 large or 3 medium SHALLOTS, peeled and thinly sliced (½ cup/55 g)

½ cup/65 g coarsely chopped DRIED CRANBERRIES

½ tsp finely grated LEMON ZEST

1 tbsp chopped or finely sliced FRESH SAGE

2 tbsp chopped TOASTED PECANS (see page 198)

FOR THE TART
FLOUR for dusting

1 disk SAVORY RUSTIC TART DOUGH (page 116)

2 tbsp plus 1 tsp coarsely grated PARMIGIANO-REGGIANO

1 tbsp finely chopped TOASTED PECANS (see page 198), plus 1 tsp

10 to 12 small fresh whole SAGE LEAVES

This little tart is a gem or, I should say, a jewel. The generous amount of cranberries makes it so sparkly and sprightly that it could pass for a savory dessert or a really, really good mincemeat pie (no lard!). I keep the cheese light on this tart, too, as I like the way the filling sort of tumbles out when you cut it and mixes with all the buttery shards of pastry. This would make a pretty and delicious addition to a buffet for a harvest party (hay ride and pumpkin carving optional). But you could also serve a wedge of this for supper alongside a warm salad like the Roasted Beet & Shallot Salad with Mint & Sopressata Crisps (page 26). Be sure to pull the dough out of the fridge while the squash is roasting.

SERVES 4

1 ***To make the egg wash:*** In a small bowl, whisk together the egg yolk and cream, cover with plastic wrap, and set aside.

2 ***To make the filling:*** Preheat the oven to 450°F/230°C/gas 8. Line a large heavy-duty rimmed baking sheet with parchment. In a medium bowl, toss the squash with the olive oil and 1 tsp salt. Transfer the squash to the prepared sheet and spread it out in a single layer. Roast the squash, flipping it over once with a spatula (if desired), until tender (the bottoms will be brown), 28 to 30 minutes.

3 ***Meanwhile, in a small heavy skillet,*** melt the butter over medium-low heat. Add the shallots and a pinch of salt and cook, stirring occasionally, until softened and golden, about 8 minutes. Add the cranberries, stir, and remove the pan from the heat. Let cool for 1 to 2 minutes and stir in the lemon zest.

4 ***Transfer the roasted squash*** to a large mixing bowl. Add the shallot-cranberry mixture and toss thoroughly but gently. Stir in the chopped sage and chopped pecans.

5 ***To make the tart:*** Reduce the oven temperature to 400°F/200°C/gas 6. Position a rack in the center of the oven. Line a large heavy-duty rimmed baking sheet with parchment.

6 ***Sprinkle your work surface*** with flour and spread it around with your hand. Put the disk of dough in front of you and lightly tap it with the rolling pin to start spreading it. Gently roll it out, lifting and giving the disk a quarter-turn after each roll, until you have a roughly 12-in/30.5-cm round. Try not to roll your pin over the edges of the dough, as that will tend to make the edges thinner than the center. (If your edges get ragged or torn, patch them back together or trim them.) If the dough is sticking, lift it up and toss a bit of flour underneath and/or over it. Roll up or drape the dough over your rolling pin, and unroll or undrape it onto the prepared baking sheet.

7 ***Sprinkle 1 tbsp of the Parmigiano*** and the 1 tbsp finely chopped pecans over the dough, leaving a 2-in/5-cm border around the edge. Pour and scrape the squash mixture into the middle of the tart. (Pile on the filling at first, then smooth it out to a relatively even mound, again leaving a 2 in/5-cm border around the edge.) Sprinkle the filling with another 1 tbsp of the Parmigiano.

8 ***Pleat and fold the edges of the dough*** up and over the outer edge of the filling all the way around the tart. (You will be folding in that 2-in/5-cm border.) You don't have to go crazy making a lot of pleats; folding in a piece of dough about every 2 to 3 in/5 to 7.5 cm around the tart will get you the results you want. (You'll have a total of eight to ten pleats.)

9 ***Brush the edges of the dough*** with the egg wash (you won't use it all). Press the whole sage leaves into the pleated dough all around the edges, and sprinkle the edges with the remaining 1 tsp Parmigiano and the remaining 1 tsp chopped pecans.

10 ***Bake until nicely golden*** all over and crisp and brown on the bottom (check with a spatula), 38 to 40 minutes. Let cool for a few minutes and use the parchment to slide the tart onto a cutting board. Let cool for another 5 to 10 minutes before slicing and serving.

Roasted Ratatouille Tart

with Goat Cheese & Mint

Long ago and far away, I worked in a busy gourmet market cooking take-out food. The fun part about this job was not making a ton of potato salad over Labor Day weekend. It was dreaming up clever items that would sell well any old day. One of my most popular creations was a savory rustic tart filled with roasted vegetables and goat cheese. Back then, I had to use pie dough that wasn't quite as yummy (or flaky) as the tart dough I prefer to use now, but the crowd-pleasing roasted filling is quite similar. It's a mix of summer ratatouille-ish vegetables, though it doesn't turn out stewlike, just pleasantly moist. It's super-easy to make but does need 45 minutes or so in the oven. You can make the filling while your dough comes to room temperature, or you can make it ahead and refrigerate it, if you like. (Bring back to room temp before using.) Serve a slice of this tart with Summer Shades of Green Side Salad with Avocado & Lime-Honey Dressing (page 191), for supper on an early autumn evening.

SERVES 4

→

FOR THE EGG WASH
1 EGG YOLK

2 tbsp HEAVY CREAM

FOR THE FILLING
6 oz/170 g medium CHERRY TOMATOES, halved (about a heaping 1 cup)

4 oz/115 g RED or YELLOW BELL PEPPER, cut into ¾-in/2-cm dice (about 1 cup)

4 oz/115 g ITALIAN (or other small) EGGPLANT, skin scored and cut into ¾-in/2-cm dice (about 1½ cups)

4 oz/115 g ZUCCHINI, cut into ½-in/12-mm dice (about 1 cup)

4 oz/115 g (about ½ medium) RED ONION, cut into ¾-in/2-cm dice (about 1 cup)

2 tbsp EXTRA-VIRGIN OLIVE OIL

KOSHER SALT

FOR THE TART
FLOUR for dusting

1 disk SAVORY RUSTIC TART DOUGH (page 116)

¼ cup/30 g) grated PARMIGIANO-REGGIANO

1 cup/115 g cold FRESH GOAT CHEESE, crumbled while still chilled

1 tbsp thinly sliced FRESH MINT

1 ***To make the egg wash:*** In a small bowl, whisk together the egg yolk and cream, cover with plastic wrap, and set aside.

2 ***To make the filling:*** Preheat the oven to 400°F/200°C/gas 6. Position a rack in the center of the oven. In a 13-by-9-in/33-by-23-cm heatproof glass baking dish (or two smaller shallow baking dishes with a total volume of about 3 qt/2.8 L), combine the cherry tomatoes, bell pepper, eggplant, zucchini, red onion, olive oil, and ½ tsp salt. Toss gently but thoroughly and spread in a single layer. Roast until the veggies have shrunk and caramelized but are still a bit moist, 45 to 55 minutes. Let cool in the baking dish.

3 ***To make the tart:*** Be sure that one oven rack is still positioned in the center of the oven. Line a large heavy-duty rimmed baking sheet with parchment.

4 ***Sprinkle your work surface*** with flour and spread it around with your hand. Put the disk of dough in front of you and lightly tap it with the rolling pin to start spreading it. Gently roll it out, lifting and giving the disk a quarter-turn after each roll, until you have a roughly 12-in/30.5-cm round. Try not to roll your pin over the edges of the dough, as that will tend to make the edges thinner than the center. (If your edges get ragged or torn, patch them back together or trim them.) If the dough is sticking, lift it up and toss a bit of flour underneath and/or over it. Roll up or drape the dough over your rolling pin, and unroll or undrape it onto the prepared baking sheet.

5 ***Sprinkle 1 tbsp of the Parmigiano*** over the dough, leaving a 2-in/5-cm border around the edge. Top the Parmigiano with half of the goat cheese, half of the mint, and half of the roasted filling, again leaving a 2-in/5-cm border. Sprinkle with 1 tbsp of the Parmigiano, and repeat with the remaining goat cheese, mint, and filling. Top with 1 tbsp of the Parmigiano.

6 ***Pleat and fold the edges of the dough*** up and over the outer edge of the filling all the way around the tart. (You will be folding in that 2-in/5-cm border.) You don't have to go crazy making a lot of pleats; folding in a piece of dough about every 2 to 3 in/5 to 7.5 cm around the tart will get you the results you want. (You'll have a total of eight to ten pleats.)

7 ***Brush the edges of the dough*** with the egg wash (you won't use it all), and sprinkle the remaining 1 tbsp Parmigiano over the edges as well as the rest of the tart.

8 ***Bake until nicely golden*** all over and crisp and brown on the bottom (check with spatula), 38 to 40 minutes. Let cool for a few minutes and use the parchment to slide the tart onto a cutting board. Let cool for another 5 to 10 minutes before slicing and serving.

Seven-Treasure Roasted Winter Veggie Tart

FOR THE EGG WASH

1 EGG YOLK

2 tbsp HEAVY CREAM

FOR THE FILLING

1 small, firm-ripe BOSC PEAR, peeled, cored, and cut into ¾-in/2-cm pieces (about 1¼ cups)

4 oz/115 g medium CREMINI or BABY BELLA MUSHROOMS, quartered or cut into sixths, if large (about 1¾ cups)

4 oz/115 g CAULIFLOWER FLORETS, cut into ¾-in/2-cm pieces (about 1⅓ cups)

½ small SWEET POTATO, unpeeled and cut into ¾-in/2-cm pieces (about 1 cup)

¼ lb/115 g unpeeled YELLOW or PURPLE POTATOES, cut into ¾-in/2-cm pieces (about ¾ cup)

3 oz/85 g CARROTS, peeled and cut into ¾-in/2-cm dice (about ½ cup)

3 small SHALLOTS (about 3 oz/85 g), quartered with stem ends kept intact and peeled

3 tbsp EXTRA-VIRGIN OLIVE OIL

1 tsp KOSHER SALT

2 tsp ORANGE JUICE

1 tsp PURE MAPLE SYRUP

1 tsp BALSAMIC VINEGAR

1 tsp chopped FRESH THYME

Sure, I'm being a bit sneaky here. I call this chock-full-o'-vegetables tart my Seven-Treasure Tart, hoping it might appeal to a few kids. Maybe there's a game in counting the seven vegetables (oops, six—one of them is a fruit) inside the tart. But even for big kids, this is a really tasty way to eat a great variety of winter veggies. We love to eat this satisfying tart (made with the same crazy-flaky crust I use for all the tarts in this chapter) with a big hearty salad and a cup of leftover Smoky Chipotle Black Bean Chili (page 50) on a cold January night. Like its cousin, the Roasted Ratatouille Tart (page 123), this one has a filling that takes a bit of time to cook. But it can be done in about the amount of time it takes for your dough to warm up out of the fridge.

SERVES 4

1 ***To make the egg wash:*** In a small bowl, whisk together the egg yolk and cream, cover with plastic wrap, and set aside.

2 ***To make the filling:*** Preheat the oven to 425°F/220°C/gas 7. In a 13-by-9-in/33-by-23-cm heatproof glass baking dish (or two smaller shallow baking dishes with a total volume of about 3 qt/2.8 L), combine the pear, all the vegetables, the olive oil, and 1 tsp salt. Toss gently but thoroughly and spread the vegetables in a single layer as best you can (the pan will seem crowded). Roast, stirring and flipping once every 20 minutes, until the veggies are tender, somewhat shrunken, and nicely browned, 50 to 55 minutes. Let cool for 10 minutes and transfer to a mixing bowl. In a small bowl, whisk together the orange juice, maple syrup, and vinegar and drizzle the mixture over the vegetables. Add the thyme and the ½ tsp rosemary, and toss.

3 ***In a small bowl,*** combine the feta and cream and mash with a fork into a paste.

4 ***To make the tart:*** Reduce the oven temperature to 400°F/200°C/gas 6. Position a rack in the center of the oven. Line a large heavy-duty rimmed baking sheet pan with parchment.

½ tsp chopped FRESH ROSEMARY, plus a little more for sprinkling

¾ cup/85 g good-quality FETA CHEESE (I like French Valbreso brand.)

3 tbsp HEAVY CREAM

FOR THE TART
FLOUR for dusting

1 disk SAVORY RUSTIC TART DOUGH (page 116)

3 tbsp plus 1 tsp grated PARMIGIANO-REGGIANO

5 ***Sprinkle your work surface*** with flour and spread it around with your hand. Put the disk of dough in front of you and lightly tap it with the rolling pin to start spreading it. Gently roll it out, lifting and giving the disk a quarter-turn after each roll, until you have a roughly 12-in/30.5-cm round. Try not to roll your pin over the edges of the dough, as that will tend to make the edges thinner than the center. (If your edges get ragged or torn, patch them back together or trim them.) If the dough is sticking, lift it up and toss a bit of flour underneath and/or over it. Roll up or drape the dough over your rolling pin, and unroll or undrape it onto the prepared baking sheet.

6 ***Sprinkle 1 tbsp of the Parmigiano*** over the dough, leaving a 2-in/5-cm border around the edge. Top the Parmigiano with half of the roasted filling and spoon half of the feta mixture over it, again leaving a 2-in/5-cm border. Sprinkle with 1 tbsp of the Parmigiano and top with the remaining roasted filling and the feta mixture. Top with 1 tbsp of the Parmigiano.

7 ***Pleat and fold the edges of the dough*** up and over the outer edge of the filling all the way around the tart. (You will be folding in that 2-in/5-cm border.) You don't have to go crazy making a lot of pleats; folding in a piece of dough about every 2 to 3 in/5 to 7.5 cm around the tart will get you the results you want. (You'll have a total of eight to ten folds.)

8 ***Brush the edges of the dough*** with the egg wash (you won't use it all), and sprinkle the remaining 1 tsp of Parmigiano and a little bit of rosemary over the edges as well as the rest of the tart.

9 ***Bake until nicely golden*** all over and crisp and brown on the bottom (check with a spatula), 38 to 40 minutes. Let cool for a few minutes and use the parchment to slide the tart onto a cutting board. Let cool for 15 minutes before slicing and serving.

CHAPTER 7

Making Veggie Sautés & Ragoûts: How It Works

A pan, the stovetop, some veggies, and you—the possibilities are ridiculous. As much as I love my oven for roasting veggies, baking pizza, finishing a frittata—so many things—there's nothing like standing at the stove and getting into it. Spoon or spatula or tongs in hand, you're stirring, you're flipping, you're turning the heat up and down, you're listening to the sizzle, watching for the browning, and pretty much enjoying the whole satisfying process of cooking.

The more you cook on the stovetop, the better cook you become, because you learn to manipulate heat and moisture to get the results you want. Cover or uncover? Heat up or down? Stir or not? Which kind of pan? You're using all your senses, moving your hands around, and gaining a sense of timing, too.

With all these things under your control, you can make some of the most delicious vegetable dishes on the stovetop. I've had to narrow the choices here; my sautés and ragoûts are just two points on the spectrum of stovetop possibilities. I even stretch the traditional definition of a French sauté beyond high heat and an uncrowded pan: For our purposes, a sauté is a mix of colorful, evenly cut vegetables cooked in a wide skillet with enough fat to keep them from drying out and to cook them through (no added liquids here). In plain English, this means we can get a variety of delicious dishes from the versatile sauté—including a quesadilla filling and a topping for polenta or rice. With each recipe, the "wide skillet" may be defined somewhat differently; the important thing is that all the veggies get plenty of contact with the direct searing heat of the pan.

For a ragoût, which defines itself by being ever so slightly saucy (but not stewy), I keep the veggies moist by cooking them in a covered Dutch oven. The high sides and lid trap moisture and help dense veggies like baby artichokes and Brussels sprouts to cook while they brown, too. I cook each veggie separately and combine them at the end, when I also add a little flavorful liquid (juices like orange, pomegranate, and lime) along with aromatics (like ginger and garlic), to make a silky pan sauce to nap the veggies. These ragoûts taste sublime, and they're just the thing to serve for an elegant all-veggie dinner, perhaps with a grain dish on the plate, too.

Sautés and ragoûts are just two ways to make the stovetop work in the veggie kitchen (of course we also have soups, pastas, and chili—just in this book!), but I encourage you to experiment. Pay close attention to your cooking equipment. If you're not getting the results you want, it's well worth your money to get a good heavy-duty sauté pan, a hefty Dutch oven, or a better-quality nonstick skillet. And get to know your stove. My medium heat may be your medium-low—or medium-high. Use all your senses and pay attention to doneness clues in the recipes: If something is browning too slowly or too fast, adjust the heat. It's all in your hands!

Double-Corn, Black Bean & Cheddar Quesadillas

FOR THE FILLING

1 tbsp UNSALTED BUTTER

1 tbsp EXTRA-VIRGIN OLIVE OIL

1 small ONION, cut into 3/8-in/2-cm dice (about 3/4 cup)

1/2 GREEN or RED BELL PEPPER, cut into 3/8-in/2-cm dice (about 1/2 cup)

KOSHER SALT

1 cup/155 g FRESH CORN KERNELS, cut from 1 1/2 medium cobs (see page 213)

1/2 tsp GROUND CUMIN

1/4 tsp GROUND CORIANDER

1/4 cup/45 g drained and rinsed canned BLACK BEANS

1/2 tsp SHERRY or CIDER VINEGAR

2 tbsp chopped FRESH CILANTRO

FOR THE QUESADILLAS

1 1/2 cups/130 g coarsely grated EXTRA-SHARP CHEDDAR

8 small WHITE CORN TORTILLAS

2 tsp UNSALTED BUTTER

4 tsp EXTRA-VIRGIN OLIVE OIL

{Sautés} I love the crispy-crunchy texture and the super-corn-y flavor of a quesadilla made with corn tortillas. Nothin' wrong with flour tortillas, but there's something totally Tijuana cool about frying up a corn-tortilla quesadilla and biting into its nacho-esque yumminess. Okay, I'll stop before you think I've lost my mind. The filling I conjured up here gets an extra hit of corn flavor from fresh corn kernels as well as a meaty boost from black beans and my favorite spice duo, cumin and coriander. The sauté includes onions and bell peppers, and while it may take a few minutes longer than your average quesadilla filling, it's worth it. (The filling is delicious outside of a quesadilla, too, served on rice or in an omelet.) Try serving these alongside Chile Rice with Green Beans & Toasted Pecans (page 155) for a totally delicious Tex-Mex supper. Making quesadillas takes a bit of patience, but stick with 'em—you'll have fun!

SERVES 4

1 ***To make the filling:*** In a medium heavy nonstick skillet, heat the butter and olive oil over medium heat. When the butter has melted, add the onion, bell pepper, and 1/4 tsp salt. Cover and cook, stirring occasionally, until the onion is translucent and the veggies are somewhat softened, about 4 minutes. Uncover and continue cooking until the vegetables are lightly browned and shrunken, another 4 to 5 minutes. Add the corn and another 1/4 tsp salt. Cook, stirring, until intensified in color, glistening, and somewhat shrunken (some will be lightly browned), 4 to 5 minutes more. Stir in the cumin and the coriander and cook until fragrant, about 30 seconds. Add the black beans and stir to incorporate. Stir in the vinegar and remove the skillet from the heat. Let the mixture cool for 15 minutes and then stir in the fresh cilantro.

→

2 ***To assemble the quesadillas:*** Arrange the corn–black bean mixture, cheese, tortillas, butter, and olive oil near your stove. In a medium or large heavy nonstick skillet, heat 1 tsp olive oil and 1/2 tsp butter over medium heat. When the oil is hot and the butter has melted, add one tortilla to the pan. Sprinkle about 2 tbsp of the cheese over it, leaving a narrow border around the outside edge. Spoon about one-quarter of the filling (a generous 1/3 cup) onto the tortilla, and sprinkle with another 2 tbsp of the cheese. Top with a second tortilla and lightly press down on it with your hand. (Push any errant bits back in with your fingers, and watch out for corn left in the pan; it can pop at you!). Cover the pan and cook until the underside is crisp and lightly browned, 2 to 3 minutes. Uncover and, using a spatula, lift the quesadilla and carefully flip it over. (You might need to use your fingertips as a guide.) Cook until the underside is crispy and lightly browned, about another 2 minutes.

3 ***Transfer the quesadilla*** to a cutting board and let it cool for a few minutes before cutting it into quarters. Repeat with the remaining tortillas and filling, using more olive oil and butter as needed with each quesadilla. (You will have a total of 16 quarters.)

Caramelized Winter Veggies

with Collard Green "Confetti"

{Sautés} It's probably no coincidence that I created this recipe in late October, when the leaves are finally turning on Martha's Vineyard, and it seems like every shade of orange—from tangerine to ochre—is flitting by my window. These are the colors in this warming, slow sauté of carrots, Yukon gold potatoes, rutabagas, and onions. It even gets a hit of green from thin ribbons of collards.

The trick with this "slow-sauté" technique is to let the vegetables steam and brown at the same time. The pan starts out pretty full, so I jump-start the steaming by covering the pan for the first 15 minutes. (The "steam" isn't added liquid but the moisture the veggies give off when cooked in a crowded pan.) But gradually, browning kicks in, and the veggies get golden and tender. Folding the collards and a bit of garlic in at the end makes a stunning finish. A flat-edge spatula is great for turning these veggies, and you'll need a large nonstick skillet with a lid. (If you don't have a lid, improvise with a sheet pan.) We love this hearty sauté atop polenta.

SERVES 3, OR 4 WITH POLENTA

2 tsp SHERRY VINEGAR

2 tsp PURE MAPLE SYRUP

4 oz/115 g COLLARD GREENS (about ½ small bunch)

3 tbsp EXTRA-VIRGIN OLIVE OIL, plus more as needed

10 oz/280 g peeled RUTABAGA*, cut into ½-in/12-mm dice

8 to 9 oz/225 to 255 g peeled CARROTS, cut into ½-in/12-mm dice

10 oz/280 g YUKON GOLD POTATOES, unpeeled and cut into ½-in/12-mm dice

KOSHER SALT

1 large ONION, cut into ½-in/12-mm dice (about 1½ cups/92 g)

1 tbsp minced GARLIC

FRESHLY GROUND PEPPER (optional)

CHEATER'S 5-MINUTE POLENTA (page 210; optional)

1 ***In a small bowl,*** combine the vinegar and maple syrup and whisk until well combined. Set aside.

2 ***Remove the stems*** from the collard leaves by holding a stem with one hand and pulling the leaves away from it with the other. Rip the leaves completely in half lengthwise. You should have about 2 oz/55 g trimmed collards. Make a stack of leaves, roll them up (lengthwise, so that you will be cutting across the leaf into short pieces), and cut them crosswise into very thin (1/4-in/6-mm) ribbons. Repeat with any remaining leaves. Set aside.

3 ***In a large nonstick skillet,*** heat the olive oil over medium-high heat. Add the rutabaga, carrots, potatoes, and 1½ tsp salt. Stir and toss well until the veggies are evenly coated with oil. (The pan will look crowded.) Reduce the heat to medium, cover partially, and cook, stirring and flipping about every 5 minutes with a flat-edged spatula, for 15 minutes. (You should see browning after about 10 minutes. Listen to the pan; you should hear a gentle sizzle, not a loud one, as the vegetables cook. If the vegetables are browning too quickly, reduce the heat a bit to maintain that gentle sizzle.) Add the onion and 1/2 tsp salt and continue to cook, uncovered, stirring and flipping more frequently as browning occurs. Reduce the heat slightly, if necessary (and add a little more oil if the pan seems dry), until the vegetables are all tender and browned, about another 15 minutes.

4 ***Fold in the garlic*** and cook until fragrant, about 30 seconds. Gradually and gently mix in the collard greens in small handfuls until they are all wilted, bright green, and well mixed with the other vegetables, about 2 minutes. (Don't add all the collards at once, or they will not get evenly dispersed.)

5 ***Remove the pan from the heat,*** taste, and season with more salt and pepper (if desired). Sprinkle with the sherry-maple mixture, stir, and serve warm atop the polenta (if you like).

*What is a rutabaga? Rutabagas are big yellow-fleshed turnips with purple and yellow skin. If you buy them at the grocery store, they will be quite large—about the size of a softball—and the skin will usually be waxed. You can find smaller, unwaxed rutabagas at some farmers' markets or natural groceries. Either way, the tough skin should be peeled or cut away: With a sharp chef's knife, trim the ends so that the root can sit flat. Then cut the skin away from top to bottom all the way around, as if you were peeling the rind from an orange.

Green Bean, Red Onion & Cherry Tomato Ragoût

with Pomegranate Pan Sauce

¼ cup/60 ml **POMEGRANATE JUICE**

2 tsp **HONEY**

1 tsp **BALSAMIC VINEGAR**

3 tbsp **UNSALTED BUTTER** (1½ tbsp cut into 6 pieces and kept chilled in the refrigerator)

2 tbsp **EXTRA-VIRGIN OLIVE OIL**

1 lb/455 g **GREEN BEANS**, trimmed and each cut into 2 or 3 pieces

KOSHER SALT

1 medium **RED ONION** (5 to 6 oz/140 to 170 g), cut lengthwise into thick slices

8 oz/225 g medium red ripe **CHERRY TOMATOES**, halved

1½ tsp minced **GARLIC**

PREPARED COUSCOUS, GRILLED BREAD (page 203), or **BUTTERY POPOVERS** (page 205) for serving (optional)

{Ragoûts} Green beans were my childhood nemesis: My mom cooked them nearly every night, my dad grew them all summer, and I just couldn't figure out how to avoid them, though I desperately wanted to. Flash-forward to last summer, and I grew green beans in my garden—tons of them! They just kept coming and coming, and I have to say I didn't mind. I really enjoy the flavor of fresh green beans, especially now that I've learned to cook them a number of different ways so that they never get boring. The method I'm using here is easy and delicious: The beans brown and steam at the same time for a wonderful flavor and texture. I decided to pair them with cherry tomatoes, red onions, and a buttery, almost sweet-and-sour pomegranate finishing sauce, so that you can enjoy these on a late-summer or early-fall night when the green beans and cherry tomatoes are both still in season. I like to serve this over couscous or with Grilled Bread on the side. Or sometimes we eat it draped over split Buttery Popovers.

SERVES 3 OR 4

1 ***In a glass measure*** or small bowl, whisk together the pomegranate juice, honey, and vinegar until the honey has dissolved.

2 ***In a large straight-sided sauté pan,*** heat 1 tbsp of the butter and 1 tbsp of the olive oil over medium heat. When the butter has melted, add the green beans and 1 tsp salt. Cover and cook, stirring frequently, until all the beans have browned in places (some will be browner than others), 13 to 15 minutes. (First they will turn bright green, and then they will begin to shrink and turn brown. Be sure to replace the lid after stirring; it retains moisture for steaming the beans.) Transfer the beans to a large plate or bowl and cover very loosely with aluminum foil. Remove the pan from the heat for a minute to let the temperature drop a bit.

3 ***Return the pan to medium-low heat*** and add the remaining 1 tbsp olive oil, the onion, and a big pinch of salt. Cover and cook, stirring frequently, until the onion is limp and lightly browned in places, 4 to 6 minutes.

4 ***Add ½ tbsp of the butter,*** the cherry tomatoes, and garlic and stir gently. Cover and cook briefly, stirring once or twice, just until the garlic is soft and fragrant and the tomatoes are heated, 45 seconds to 1 minute. Transfer the cherry tomato–onion mixture to a bowl (separate from the green beans).

5 ***Raise the heat to medium-high*** and pour the pomegranate juice mixture into the pan. Cook, uncovered, until the liquids have thickened somewhat and reduced to about 3 tbsp, 2 to 2½ minutes. (There will be a thin layer of bubbling sauce across the bottom of the pan.) Remove the pan from the heat and stir in the cold butter, a few pieces at a time, just until melted and creamy.

6 ***Return the green beans to the pan*** and toss with the sauce. Stir in the tomato-onion mixture very gently. Transfer the ragoût to a serving platter or divide among individual plates. Serve over couscous or along with the bread or popovers (if desired).

Spring Veggie Ragoût

with Baby Artichokes, Fingerling Potatoes & Spinach

1½ LEMONS

9 BABY ARTICHOKES

3 tbsp UNSALTED BUTTER

2 tbsp EXTRA-VIRGIN OLIVE OIL

KOSHER SALT

¾ lb/340 g small FINGERLING POTATOES, cut in half lengthwise and, if longer than 2 in/5 cm, cut in half again crosswise

1½ tsp minced GARLIC

2 tsp chopped FRESH THYME

2 oz/55 g BABY SPINACH LEAVES (stems removed, if necessary)

3 tbsp HEAVY CREAM

½ tsp SHERRY VINEGAR

FRESHLY GROUND PEPPER (optional)

{Ragoûts} "If only, if only," I keep saying. If only people knew how easy baby artichokes are to prepare, they'd be cooking them like crazy. The darn things are so tasty, and really—I swear—they take only minutes to prep. (There's no messy choke inside, like in older artichokes.) They're so meaty, too. Filling and full of deep flavor. Whenever they're around, they make any veggie dish feel more like a main event. In this stovetop ragoût, I quickly braise and brown them—as well as one of my other all-time favorite veggies, fingerling potatoes—before finishing the combo by folding in some baby spinach, garlic, fresh thyme, and a bit of cream. The dish is just slightly saucy (which makes a ragoût a ragoût and not a stew!) and so flavorful that it really can't be stretched. This is a recipe for two. Kinda romantic. Well, maybe three, if you insist. Because this would be nice with a little roast chicken on the side, too.

SERVES 2 OR 3

1 ***Fill a medium bowl half full of water.*** Halve the whole lemon, squeeze the juice from the two halves into the water, and drop the lemon halves into the lemon water. Cut the stems off the artichokes at the base. Working with one artichoke at a time, peel away all the outer leaves until you are left with a (somewhat cone-shaped) mostly lemon-lime-colored artichoke with the top third still light green. With a sharp knife, cut about 3/4 in/2 cm off the top and, with a paring knife, clean up the stem end just a bit. (Don't remove too much; that's the tasty heart.) Quarter the artichoke lengthwise. Rub the cut sides of each piece with the remaining lemon half and drop the artichoke quarters into the lemon water.

2 ***In a large Dutch oven*** or other deep, wide pan, heat 1 tbsp of the butter and 1 tbsp of the olive oil over medium-low heat. When the butter has melted, add the artichoke quarters (with whatever water still clings to them) and ½ tsp salt, cover, and cook, stirring occasionally, for 10 minutes. (The artichokes will simmer at first, and then the liquid will begin to reduce. If they begin to brown, reduce the heat.) Add 1/2 tbsp of the butter, raise the heat to medium, and continue cooking, uncovered, stirring more frequently (but gently) as the artichokes begin to brown. (Pay close attention; once the browning starts, it goes quickly.) Cook until all the artichoke pieces have some golden-brown spots on them and the bottom of the pan is brown (but do not let it blacken), 5 to 7 minutes more. Transfer the artichokes to a plate and take the pan off the heat for a moment.

3 ***Return the pan to medium-low heat*** and add 1 tbsp of the butter and the remaining olive oil to the pan. When the butter has melted, add the fingerlings, cut-side down, and season them with 3/4 tsp salt. Cover loosely and cook, without stirring, until the potato pieces are a deep golden brown on the bottom, 5 to 7 minutes. Add 3/4 cup/180 ml water to the pan and bring to a boil. Reduce to a simmer, cover loosely, and cook until the potatoes are tender and the liquid has reduced to 2 to 3 tbsp, 10 to 12 minutes.

4 ***Reduce the heat to low.*** Add the remaining 1/2 tbsp butter, the garlic, thyme, spinach, cream, reserved artichokes, and a pinch of salt to the pan and stir gently to mix. Cover and cook for 1 minute to let the spinach wilt and the liquids reduce just a bit. Uncover and remove the pan from the heat. Add the sherry vinegar, toss the ragoût, and taste. Season with more salt and freshly ground pepper (if desired). Serve right away.

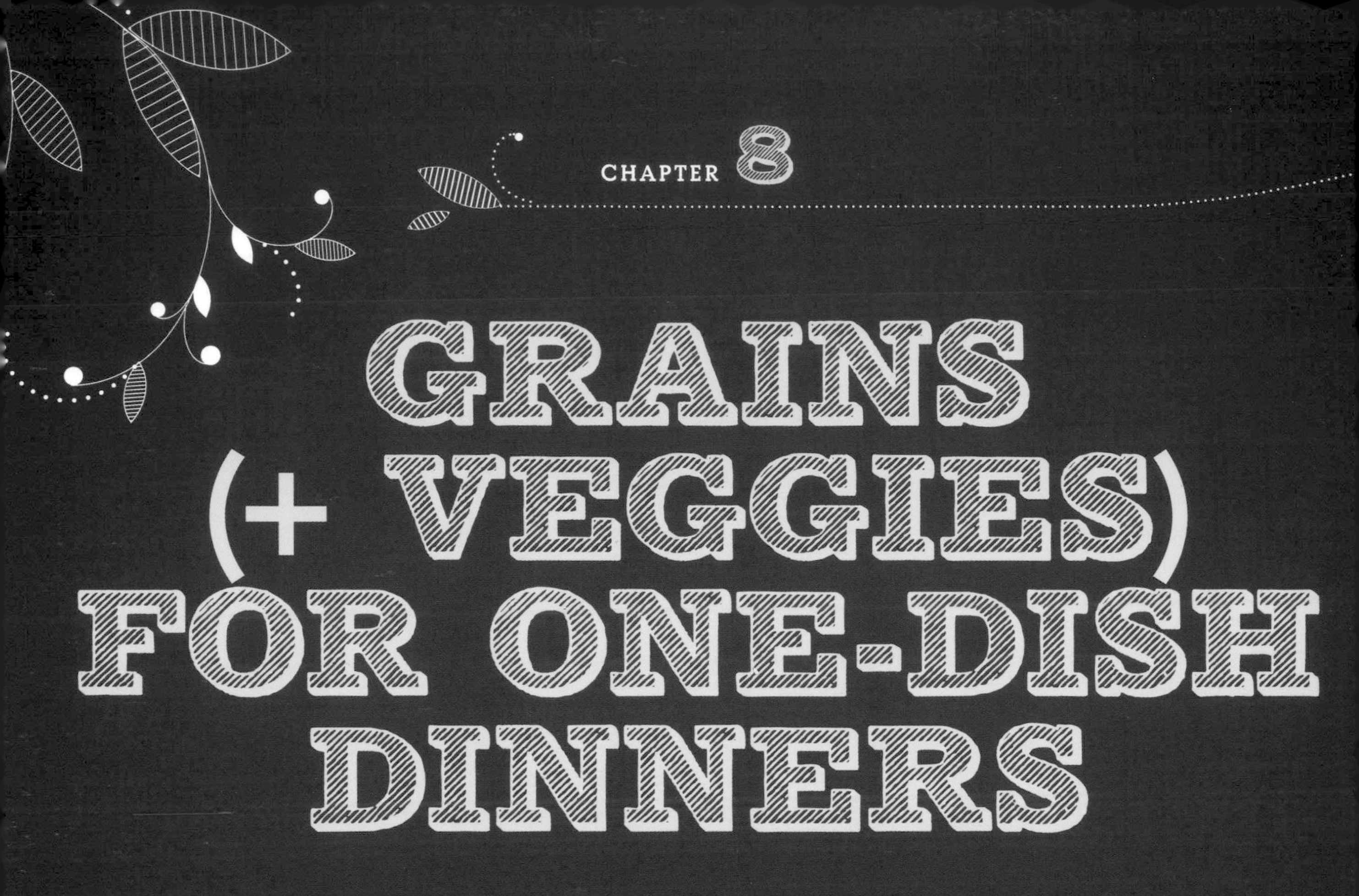

CHAPTER 8

GRAINS (+ VEGGIES) FOR ONE-DISH DINNERS

Cooking Grains (+ Veggies) for One-Dish Dinners: **How It Works**

How satisfying it is to see lined up in your pantry a row of mason jars with thousands of little grains nestled neatly like sand pebbles in each plump jar. At least that's what my ideal pantry looks like! In reality, my pantry shelves are jammed with bags and boxes of all different kinds of grains: wheat berries, farro, quinoa, millet, bulghur, and rices from basmati and jasmati to short grain and sushi. I love to cook with these darn things, so I won't be stopping the influx anytime soon. (Obviously, I have a fun organizing project ahead of me.)

If you haven't gone down this road yet, I encourage you to dabble. Try one or two of the grain recipes in this chapter to see what you think. I made a special effort here to pick a vegetable (or two) that pairs well with each grain (or rice). And then I designed recipes that would, in most cases, make satisfying one-bowl suppers for vegetarians (or for me on a nonmeat night) and that would also make fantastic main dishes with grilled or roasted meat or fish on the side.

Veggies and grains were made to go together (both share earthy, nutty, and even sweet nuances), so pairing them wasn't hard: wheat berries + Brussels sprouts; basmati + cauliflower; farro + mushrooms; quinoa + sugar snap peas. The fun part was enhancing the pairings with fresh herbs, toasted nuts, dried fruit, and flavorful sauces. For example, I love what nutty short-grain brown rice does with sweet stir-fried carrots, and not to gild the lily, for brightness and depth, I added ginger, garlic, fresh mint, fresh lime, and toasted almonds to this combo. A bit of butter carries the flavors and wraps itself around the whole dish. Yum.

I've also made an effort here to offer you the easiest way to cook each grain. Some grains, like wheat berries, farro, and short-grain brown rice, cook best in boiling water, pasta-style. After draining, you simply return them to the pot off the heat for a few minutes so excess water can evaporate. (In a pinch, you can do this ahead and gently reheat.) Other grains, like quinoa and most long-grain white rices, cook best pilaf-style, covered, in a measured amount of water. Follow the individual cooking tips closely in each recipe for the best results.

But back to stocking that pantry. When shopping, you'll see grains packaged in boxes and bags as well as loose in bins. Natural-food stores (and the loose bins) may offer a better selection, but no matter where you shop, read the packaging (or the bin label) carefully. Many grains are offered in a few different forms, each with a different cooking time. While you're stocking up, don't forget nuts and dried fruit like cranberries, raisins, and apricots. Toast some of the nuts when you get home, and keep them at the ready in the fridge. With a well-stocked pantry (and fridge), delicious one-bowl grain-and-veggie dinners could get to be a habit. Better make sure those pantry shelves are sturdy!

Warm Wheat Berries

with Roasted Brussels Sprouts, Toasted Walnuts & Dried Cranberries

This warm wheat berry dish, dressed up with dried cranberries, toasted walnuts, and a delicious tangy butter sauce, makes a great destination for nutty roasted Brussels sprouts. I've always loved the taste and texture of wheat berries, but their cooking time (usually 60 to 70 minutes but sometimes up to 80 or 90 minutes) used to frustrate me. But now I've learned that I can cook them ahead and keep them in the fridge. Then all I have to do is gently warm them back up to use in this or any similar dish. I've also recently learned—from one of my testers—that parboiled wheat berries are on the market. (They take only 15 minutes to cook!) I wouldn't choose to buy these, as I don't think the texture would be as nice. But read packages carefully; if you wind up with them, adjust your cooking time accordingly. If you decide to make this recipe in one stretch, just wait to cook the Brussels sprouts until the wheat berries have been cooking for at least 50 minutes. Bringing the two together with the sauce happens quickly at the end. Serve alongside a cup of Southwestern Spiced Butternut Squash & Apple Soup with Lime, Yogurt & Cilantro (page 34).

SERVES 3 OR 4

→

Fragrant Basmati Rice Pilaf

with Roasted Cauliflower, Chickpeas, Raisins & Golden Shallots

1/3 cup/50 g DARK RAISINS

5 tbsp/80 ml CANOLA OIL

2 1/2 tbsp UNSALTED BUTTER

3 large or 4 small SHALLOTS, thinly sliced (about 1 cup)

KOSHER SALT

1 1/2 tsp GARAM MASALA

1 cup/185 g INDIAN BASMATI RICE, rinsed

3/4 cup/120 g canned CHICKPEAS, drained and rinsed

1 lb/455 g CAULIFLOWER FLORETS, each about 1 1/2 in/4 cm long, with one flat side

2 tsp chopped GARLIC

2 tsp chopped FRESH GINGER

1/2 tsp freshly squeezed LEMON JUICE

2 tbsp chopped FRESH CILANTRO or PARSLEY

1/4 cup/30 g chopped TOASTED ALMONDS (see page 198)

4 LEMON WEDGES (optional)

When I was a very young New Yorker living on a very tiny editorial assistant's salary in a very tiny apartment, I loved to go down to East Sixth Street to eat at the Indian restaurants. Very affordable! I first met basmati rice there, and I still love its fluffy fragrant personality. For this chapter, I knew I'd want to combine it with another Indian staple, cauliflower. Roasted cauliflower, golden-brown shallots, spices, cilantro, raisins, chickpeas, and toasted almonds—I knew that combo would do right by basmati. The spice I use is actually an Indian blend called garam masala, which is now available in grocery stores and online. Spicy, sweet, sultry—garam masala has all kinds of graceful nuances from different spices, including cinnamon, cardamom, cumin, coriander, cloves, ginger, and more. I prefer imported Indian basmati to American. Find it in the bulk grain section of the grocery or in burlap bags in the packaged rice section. (Carolina Rice packages imported Indian basmati.) One tip: If you pop the cauliflower into the oven just after you start cooking the rice, the two will be ready at the same time.

SERVES 4

1 ***Preheat the oven to 450°F/230°C/gas 8.*** Line a large, heavy-duty rimmed baking sheet with parchment. Put the raisins in a small bowl and pour 3 tbsp boiling water over them.

2 ***Combine 1 tbsp of the canola oil*** and 1 tbsp of the butter in a 2- or 2 1/2-qt/2- or 2.4-L nonstick saucepan over medium-low heat. Add the shallots and a good pinch of salt and cook, stirring, until very soft, about 10 minutes. Raise the heat to medium (or just shy of medium-high) and continue to cook, stirring frequently, until the shallots are browned (many will be crispy, too), another 6 to 8 minutes. (Watch carefully; the browning will go more quickly at the end.) With a slotted spoon, transfer the shallots to a plate.

3 ***Reduce the heat to medium-low.*** Add ½ tbsp of the butter to the pan. When it has melted, add 3/4 tsp of the garam masala and stir well (it will bubble up). Add the rice, chickpeas, and 1 1/4 tsp salt to the saucepan and stir well. Stir in 1 3/4 cups/ 420 ml water and bring to a boil. Reduce to a very low simmer, cover, and cook for 20 minutes. Remove from the heat and let the rice sit for 5 minutes, then fluff with a fork. (The chickpeas and spices will have risen to the top.)

4 ***In a medium mixing bowl,*** toss the cauliflower with 3 tbsp of the canola oil and 3/4 tsp salt. Spread the florets (cut-side down) in a single layer on the baking sheet. Roast until tender and well browned on the bottoms, 20 to 22 minutes.

5 ***In a small skillet,*** heat the remaining 1 tbsp butter and the remaining 1 tbsp canola oil over medium heat. When the butter has melted, add the garlic and ginger and cook, stirring, until softened and fragrant, 30 seconds to 1 minute. Add the remaining 3/4 tsp garam masala and stir well. Remove the skillet from the heat and add the lemon juice, and the raisins and all their liquid to the skillet. Stir well.

6 ***Using a fork,*** transfer the rice and chickpeas to a large mixing bowl, fluffing the rice again in the process. Add the cauliflower to the bowl. Drizzle and scrape the contents of the skillet over the rice and veggies and stir well but gently. Add the cilantro and almonds and stir again. Taste and add more salt, if necessary. Serve right away, garnished with the golden shallots and with the lemon wedges (for light squeezing only!) (if desired).

Chile Rice

with Green Beans & Toasted Pecans

South meets West in this inspired bowl-o-rama. (A bowl-o-rama is my idea of something fun to plunk in your lap and eat in front of the TV.) A favorite Southern combination—green beans and pecans—meets the warming Western flavors of chili spices, lime, and cilantro. (Short of a trail ride and a live oak, you need a good John Wayne movie for this one.) The toasted pecans give this dish a great texture, and the spices, onions, garlic, lime, and cilantro work together smartly. (The milk in the cooking liquid is a traditional Mexican approach.) But I really like the personality that the sautéed green beans add to the dish. It's all about the vegetable around here, after all, and I invented this rice to show off the green beans we grew in our garden last year that just kept growing and growing . . . and growing. By the way, if you're hankering for meat, think ribs or a piece of barbecued chicken on the side for this one.

SERVES 4

→

1 tsp GROUND CUMIN

1 tsp GROUND CORIANDER

1 tsp GROUND ANCHO CHILE

½ tsp PAPRIKA

½ tsp GROUND CINNAMON

KOSHER SALT

1 cup/240 ml MILK

¾ cup/180 ml WATER or LOWER-SODIUM CHICKEN BROTH

2 tbsp UNSALTED BUTTER

2 tbsp EXTRA-VIRGIN OLIVE OIL

1 large ONION, cut into ½-in/12-mm dice

2 tsp minced GARLIC

1 cup/185 g LONG-GRAIN WHITE RICE

1 lb/455 g medium GREEN BEANS, trimmed and cut crosswise into ½-in-/12-mm-long pieces

½ cup/60 g chopped TOASTED PECANS (see page 198)

⅓ cup/10 g chopped FRESH CILANTRO

2 tsp freshly squeezed LIME JUICE, plus more if desired

1½ tsp PURE MAPLE SYRUP

½ LIME, cut into 4 wedges

1 ***In a small bowl,*** combine the cumin, coriander, ancho chile, paprika, cinnamon, and 1/4 tsp salt. In a liquid measure, combine the milk and water.

2 ***In a medium saucepan*** (that has a lid), heat 1 tbsp of the butter and 1 tbsp of the olive oil over medium-low heat. When the butter has melted, add the onion and 1/4 tsp salt, cover, and cook, stirring occasionally, until softened and translucent, 5 to 7 minutes. Uncover, raise the heat to medium, and continue to cook, stirring, until lightly browned, 7 to 8 minutes more. Reduce the heat to medium-low, add the garlic, and cook, stirring, until fragrant, about 30 seconds. Add the spice mixture and cook, stirring, until the spices are fragrant, about 30 seconds. Add all the rice and about a quarter of the milk mixture and stir, mixing well and scraping all the spices from the bottom of the pan.

3 ***Add the remaining milk mixture*** and bring to a boil. Reduce the heat to very low, cover tightly, and cook for 20 minutes.

4 ***Meanwhile, in a heavy nonstick medium skillet,*** heat the remaining 1 tbsp butter and the remaining 1 tbsp olive oil over medium-high heat. When the butter has melted, add the green beans and 1/2 tsp salt. The pan will look full. (That's okay; the beans will steam and brown at the same time.) Cook, stirring only occasionally at first and more frequently as the beans begin to brown, until the green beans have shrunk somewhat, all have a bit of browning, and some are dark brown, 9 to 12 minutes. Remove the skillet from the heat and transfer the beans to a plate.

5 ***Remove the rice pot from the heat*** and place a folded paper towel under the lid. Let sit, covered, for 5 minutes. Uncover (the foam from the milk will be on top of the rice) and fluff and stir with a fork. Re-cover loosely with the lid (leaving the paper towel in place) and let sit for 5 minutes more. Uncover and transfer the rice to a medium bowl. Stir in all the beans, three-quarters of the toasted pecans, and three-quarters of the cilantro.

6 ***In a small cup,*** combine the lime juice and maple syrup. Pour the mixture over the rice, and stir to combine. Taste the rice and season with more salt, if needed. You can also add a bit more lime, if you like. Divide the rice among four bowls and serve garnished with the remaining pecans, cilantro, and lime wedges.

TIP: When measuring liquid, be sure to view the liquid measure at eye level (bend down!). The view from above is distorted; and you could wind up using more liquid than you want.

Farro

with Balsamic-Rosemary-Roasted Shallots & Grapes over Roasted Portobellos

The ancient Tuscan grain known as farro sounds exotic but really couldn't be friendlier. Think of it as barley-esque, only sexier. Like barley, farro is often "pearled" (or "semipearled") to remove the outer husk. I like semipearled, which cooks in about 30 minutes, but check labels carefully. Fully pearled farro will cook more quickly; farro that isn't pearled at all will need about 50 minutes. When tender, the grains will be a bit exploded, like barley. Because of farro's Italian roots, I've used a lovely Italian treat—roasted grapes and shallots—as well as a balsamic-rosemary marinade to marry the farro with roasted portobello caps. The finished dish is earthy, sweet, and tart all at once, and looks lovely at the center of the plate, garnished with a rosemary sprig. Add a little something green to the plate, like sautéed spinach or escarole. For meat lovers, this would be fabulous with roast duck. Pay close attention to the timing in this recipe, which is designed to bring everything together at the same time. The shallots and grapes cook for 40 minutes; the mushrooms marinate for 20 and then cook for 20; and the farro cooks for about 30.

SERVES 4

6 tbsp/90 ml EXTRA-VIRGIN OLIVE OIL, plus extra for greasing the baking dishes

2 tbsp BALSAMIC VINEGAR

2 tsp HONEY

1 tbsp chopped FRESH ROSEMARY, plus 4 sprigs for garnish

2 tsp minced GARLIC

KOSHER SALT

2 cups/345 g large, plump SEEDLESS RED GRAPES

4 large SHALLOTS, peeled, halved, and cut lengthwise into 3/8- to 1/2-in/1-cm- to 12-mm-wide slices

4 large PORTOBELLO MUSHROOMS (about 4 oz/115 g each with the stem), stemmed and gills scraped out with a spoon

1 cup/180 g SEMIPEARLED FARRO

1 ***Preheat the oven to 425°F/220°C/gas 7.*** In a glass liquid measure or glass jar, combine the 6 tbsp/90 ml olive oil, the vinegar, honey, 2 tsp of the rosemary, the garlic, and 1/2 tsp salt. Whisk or shake well to combine.

2 ***Rub a shallow 11-by-7-in/28-by-17-cm baking dish*** with olive oil and combine the grapes and the shallots and season with a big pinch of salt. Rub a 13-by-9-in/33-by-23-cm baking dish with olive oil and arrange the portobello caps, stem-side up, in a single layer and season each cap with a pinch of salt. Pour 1 tbsp of the dressing inside and around the edges of each of the mushroom caps (for a total of 4 tbsp/60 ml). Let the mushrooms marinate for 20 minutes.

3 ***Drizzle 2 tbsp of the dressing*** over the grapes and shallots and toss to coat. (Reserve the remaining dressing.) Roast the grapes and shallots, stirring once or twice, until soft and browned, about 40 minutes. (The liquid on the bottom of the pan will be somewhat syrupy.)

4 ***Meanwhile, fill a large pasta pot*** three-quarters full of water and bring to a boil. Rinse the farro in a colander. Add 1 tsp salt and the farro to the boiling water and cook at a rapid simmer or low boil, partially covered, until the grains are tender (they will look "popped"), about 30 minutes. Drain in a colander, return to the pot (off the heat), and cover to keep warm.

5 ***When the grapes and shallots have been roasting for 20 minutes,*** put the portobello caps in the oven and roast for 20 minutes. (The edges of the mushrooms may have flattened out; they will have lost some volume; and liquid may be bubbling on top of them. The bottoms will be brown, too, and they will be cooked through.)

6 ***Transfer each of the mushroom caps,*** keeping them stem-side up, to an individual warm plate or a warm platter. (If there are any juices remaining in the pan, drizzle them over the mushrooms.) Transfer the farro to a medium mixing bowl and season it with 1/4 tsp salt. Stir in the roasted grapes and shallots (be sure to scrape out all of the pan juices), the remaining 1 tsp rosemary, and 1 to 2 tbsp of the remaining dressing. Taste and season with more salt, if necessary. Spoon the mixture evenly over each of the mushrooms.* Garnish each serving with a rosemary sprig and serve right away.

*For a nicer presentation, use a smaller amount of the farro mixture and mound it completely in the center of the mushroom with just the edges of the mushroom peeking out and the rosemary sprig leaning against the mound. You'll have extra farro, but it reheats well. Surround the mushroom with dressed cooked or raw greens.

Easy Quinoa

with Apricots, Toasted Pine Nuts & Sugar Snap Peas for Two

1 tsp freshly squeezed LIME JUICE

1 tsp HONEY

1/4 tsp GROUND CINNAMON

1/8 tsp GROUND CUMIN

1/8 tsp GROUND CORIANDER

KOSHER SALT

2 tbsp UNSALTED BUTTER

1/3 cup/30 g thinly sliced SCALLIONS (white and green parts)

3/4 cup/130 g WHITE QUINOA, rinsed well if not prerinsed

1/3 cup/65 g diced DRIED APRICOTS

1 1/4 cups/300 ml LOW-SODIUM CHICKEN BROTH or WATER

1 tsp EXTRA-VIRGIN OLIVE OIL

4 oz/115 g SUGAR SNAP PEAS, tails trimmed and each cut into 2 or 3 pieces

2 tbsp chopped FRESH CILANTRO

4 tbsp/35 g coarsely chopped TOASTED PINE NUTS (see page 198)

Quinoa is one cool grain. Well, actually, it's a seed; regardless, this tasty staple is a complete protein, gluten-free, and quick cooking. It has something for everyone. And it takes well to many different flavors, including the Middle Eastern–inspired combo here, which includes cinnamon, apricots, and pine nuts. This quick dish for two also features one of my favorite (and quickest-cooking) veggies, sugar snap peas. Sautéed for just a few minutes, the sugar snaps take on a nutty flavor that snuggles right up with the quinoa. Sometimes I sauté sugar snaps with a little diced ham or salami; you could add one of these here if you like. Or you could serve this dish with a steamed artichoke or with one of the veggie ragoûts in chapter 7. When you buy quinoa these days, most of it has been prerinsed, but check the label on the box. If you buy it in bulk and aren't sure, rinse it thoroughly before cooking to remove the soapy substance that coats the grains.

SERVES 2

1 ***In a small bowl,*** combine the lime juice and honey and set aside. In another small bowl, combine the cinnamon, cumin, coriander, and 1/2 tsp salt.

2 ***In a large saucepan,*** melt the butter over low heat. Add the scallions, cover, and cook until softened, about 3 minutes. Uncover, add the spice mixture, and stir well. Add the quinoa and apricots and stir well again to break up the apricots a bit and to distribute the quinoa. Add the broth and bring to a boil. Reduce the heat to a gentle simmer, cover, and cook until the grain is tender, the germ has separated from the seed (it will look like a ring), and the water has been absorbed, about 18 minutes. (The top layer may look less cooked than the grains underneath it; that's okay.) Remove the pot from the heat, uncover, and stir briefly, folding the top layer into the rest of the grain. Put a folded paper towel over the quinoa and replace the lid. (This will absorb a bit more moisture.) Let sit, covered, for 5 minutes. Uncover and fluff with a fork. Transfer the quinoa to a mixing bowl.

3 ***In a medium heavy nonstick skillet,*** heat the olive oil over medium heat. When the oil is hot, add the sugar snap peas, season them with 1/4 tsp salt, and toss well. Cook, stirring occasionally, until the peas turn bright green, blister, and then brown in spots all over, about 5 minutes total.

4 ***Add the snap peas,*** cilantro, 2 tbsp of the pine nuts, and half of the lime-honey mixture to the quinoa. Stir well and taste. Season with the remaining lime-honey mixture and/or more salt, if necessary. Serve right away, garnished with the remaining 2 tbsp pine nuts.

CHAPTER 9

PIZZA FOR DINNER

Making Pizza for Dinner: How It Works

The fun factor skyrockets when it comes to cooking pizza at home. I know I'm always saying that this or that recipe (this tart, that chili, this gratin) is the most fun thing to make with vegetables in the kitchen; and, truthfully, I do have trouble deciding what I like best sometimes, but there's no dish like pizza for getting everyone involved in making dinner, no other dish that's so communal and so tactile, too. Playing with the dough, rolling it out, putting on the toppings—it's a kick. In our house, my partner, Roy, is the "oven man," and his nine-year-old daughter, Libby, is the topping master. Roy's job (which he takes seriously) is to slide the pizza in and out of the oven with the peel, while singing a funny Italian song *(la-la-la, la-la-la, la-la-la-la-LAAA!)* at the top of his lungs.

And that's just when we're cooking pizza in the oven. When we move outside to the grill, it's a whole 'nother story. I learned to grill pizza when I worked in the kitchen of Al Forno restaurant in Providence, Rhode Island, many years ago. I'd never been so excited about learning to cook something, and the thrill hasn't worn off yet. I know when I'm getting ready to light the grill for pizza that it means I have good friends and family around to help me make it and eat it. And I know that a mouthful of that crispy, smoky crust is just moments away. In fact, I love grilling pizza so much—and it's such an amazing showcase for vegetables—that I wouldn't have written this book without this chapter. (My favorite: Summer-on-a-Pizza with Corn, Tomatoes & Arugula.)

Baked or grilled, my ace-in-the-hole for great pizza is a really easy, really tasty, make-ahead food-processor dough. It stores well in the fridge or freezer, and it also proofs in an hour if you want pizza tonight. I created a pizza sauce for this book, because I've never been a fan of overly seasoned "red" sauces. Mine is a delicious purée of quick-roasted plum tomatoes and was a big hit with testers and tasters. You can make it and freeze it to have on hand. Or you could, of course, use store-bought sauce. (Just don't tell me!) Or make a white pizza, like the Potato Carpaccio Pizza with Gruyère & Rosemary.

For the baked pizzas, you'll need a pizza stone, and you'll want it to be good and hot by cooking time. (Preheat the stone and the oven for an hour.) If you happen to have two stones, you can bake two pizzas at once. The stones can be placed side by side or on separate racks. A pizza peel is handy, too, but if you don't have one, you can improvise with the back of a sheet pan sprinkled with corn meal. (It works.)

For the grilled pizzas, be sure to read the recipes thoroughly before starting. I've included tips to make your grilled pizza experiences as fun as possible. There's a learning curve, but it's a fast one. So make a batch of dough, fire up the grill, and get started.

Easy Food-Processor Pizza Dough

1 lb 2 oz/510 g ALL-PURPOSE FLOUR (I like King Arthur), plus a little more for dusting

3 tbsp EXTRA-VIRGIN OLIVE OIL, plus more for the baking sheet, if making grilled pizza

1½ tsp TABLE SALT

1⅓ cups/315 ml very warm (110°F/45°C) WATER (see tip, page 156)

1 package (2¼ tsp) ACTIVE DRY YEAST

I learned to make pizza dough in the food processor when I did a story with L.A. chef Evan Kleiman years ago when I was first starting out at *Fine Cooking* magazine. That story changed my life! Once I found out how quick and easy this method was, pizza started making a much more regular appearance at our house. The great thing about fresh pizza dough is that you can immediately freeze it for future use or refrigerate it to use the next day. And if you want it *now*, as I usually do, this recipe is particularly friendly: It takes only 15 minutes to make the dough and only about 50 minutes for it to rise—just enough time to make your toppings. This dough works equally well for both pizza cooked in the oven and pizza cooked on the grill. You can replace up to one-quarter (or 4½ oz/130 g) of the all-purpose flour with whole-wheat flour. The crust will be a bit more crackerlike but still delicious. Either way, be sure to weigh your flour for the best results.

MAKES ENOUGH DOUGH FOR 4 INDIVIDUAL BAKED OR GRILLED PIZZAS

1 ***Set up a standard-sized food processor*** near a large cutting board or other work surface. (Fit the food processor with the regular chopping blade; if you have a dough blade, that will work too, but it is not necessary.) Dust the surface of your work area with all-purpose flour and have ready a little more flour. Put a bench knife (also called a dough scraper) or a chef's knife near your work area to cut the dough into pieces. Also, put a sheet pan nearby for the finished dough balls. If you're making pizza for the oven, dust the sheet pan lightly with flour. If you're making pizza for the grill, drizzle it with 1 or 2 tbsps of olive oil.

2 ***In the bowl of the food processor,*** pulse the flour and salt a few times to combine. In a glass liquid measure, combine the warm water and the yeast. Stir to partially dissolve the yeast. Add the 3 tbsp olive oil to the water-yeast mixture. With the food processor running, slowly but steadily pour the liquids through the feed tube until the dough comes together in a ball. Pulse a few extra times to incorporate the liquid fully.

3 ***Turn the dough out onto the lightly floured work surface.*** If it's a bit sticky, toss some flour over it, scrape under it with your bench knife, and toss a little flour underneath. Dust your hands with flour, too, to make handling the dough easier. Knead the dough two or three times, just until it comes together in a mass. Using the bench knife or a chef's knife, cut the dough into four equal pieces. (If you like, you can weigh the dough to make sure the four pieces are roughly even. Each should weigh about 7½ oz/215 g).

4 ***Knead each piece of dough briefly*** to push some air out and roll each into a tight, smooth ball (see Tech Tip, below). You do not need to knead for long; the food processor has done most of the work for you. Place the dough balls a little bit apart on the prepared sheet pan and either dust lightly with more flour and cover with a dish towel (for oven pizza) or drizzle and coat with a little olive oil and cover lightly with a sheet of plastic wrap (for grilled pizza). For oven pizza, let the dough balls sit until they have nearly doubled in size, 45 to 55 minutes. For grilled pizza, allow the dough to proof 10 to 15 minutes longer.

Alternatively, if you want to make pizza another day, you can put each dough ball in an individual zip-top bag and refrigerate. (Be sure to do this before the dough starts to rise. Coat the bags and the dough balls lightly with flour if you'll be baking or with oil if you'll be grilling.) Use the dough in the next 24 hours, and bring it to room temperature before using. (This will take 50 to 90 minutes, depending on your room temperature. The dough will rise as it warms up.) You can also freeze the dough right away in individual zip-top bags. Defrost in the refrigerator the night before using.

5 ***Proceed with your chosen recipe as directed.***

TECH TIP: HOW TO MAKE SMOOTH, TIGHT DOUGH BALLS

Once you have made the dough and divided it into four pieces, it only takes 1 or 2 minutes to shape each piece into a ball by kneading briefly. Start by putting one piece on your work surface and dusting it and your hands lightly with flour. With the heel of one hand, press the dough away from you; then press it again with the heel of the other hand. Fold the dough back over on itself and give it a quarter-turn. Quickly repeat the pressing and folding three or four more times. You will feel the dough tighten up. After your last fold, cup the dough in both hands and pull the dough gently down on the sides, tucking the excess underneath so that the crease—or fold—is at the bottom of the ball. Plop it on the (lightly floured or oiled) sheet pan, and you're done. If that doesn't make sense, remember kindergarten and your clay-making days, and proceed to make a ball of dough any way you can—it's pretty forgiving! (Repeat with the three remaining pieces of dough.)

Quick-Roasted Plum Tomato Pizza Sauce

I'm kind of a roasted-tomato nut, so it was perfectly natural for me to decide to purée roasted tomatoes to make pizza sauce. I don't generally love red sauces on pizza. Mostly that's because I often find the red sauce to be heavy and overseasoned. So I really wanted to create a homemade version that I'd like, and I was thrilled when this turned out to be so tasty. (It's great with pasta, too! See page 73.) I adapted this recipe from one in the "quick" roasting chapter of *Fast, Fresh & Green*, so the good news is that the tomatoes for the sauce cook in less than 45 minutes, and it only takes a minute or two to purée them in a food processor. You can make this sauce ahead, too, and keep it in the fridge for several days or in the freezer for several weeks. This recipe yields plenty for one batch of four individual baked pizzas, but if you want to make more, you can easily double it or add more tomatoes to make a bigger batch.

MAKES 1¼ TO 1¾ CUPS/300 TO 420 ML, OR ENOUGH FOR 6 INDIVIDUAL OVEN-BAKED PIZZAS, 4 INDIVIDUAL GRILLED PIZZAS, OR 1 CLASSIC BAKED PASTA FOR TWO

1 tbsp EXTRA-VIRGIN OLIVE OIL, plus ¼ cup/60 ml

2 to 2¼ lb/910 g to 1 kg PLUM TOMATOES

KOSHER SALT

SUGAR

1½ tsp FRESH THYME

1 scant tbsp FRESH OREGANO (torn if large)

1½ tsp BALSAMIC VINEGAR, plus more if needed

2 medium GARLIC CLOVES, cut crosswise into very thin slices

1 ***Preheat the oven to 425°F/220°C/gas 7.*** Line a large, heavy-duty, rimmed baking sheet with aluminum foil and cover the foil with parchment. Brush the parchment with the 1 tbsp olive oil.

2 ***Halve each tomato lengthwise,*** and, leaving in the core, scrape out the seeds and ribs with a melon baller or measuring spoon. Put the tomato halves, cut-side up, on the parchment.

3 ***Season the cavity of each tomato*** half with a small pinch of salt and a big pinch of sugar. Tuck the thyme and oregano leaves into the cavities, distributing them evenly among the halves. Drizzle a few drops of the vinegar inside each tomato half. (It's easiest to put a little vinegar in a small bowl and use a small measuring spoon, like a ⅛ tsp, to distribute a few drops to each tomato.) Drop a slice or two of garlic into each cavity. Drizzle the remaining olive oil in and around the tops of each tomato, distributing the oil evenly.

4 ***Roast the tomatoes*** until they are wrinkled and somewhat collapsed, 40 to 45 minutes. The bottoms will be lightly browned, and the tomatoes will collapse more as they cool.

5 ***Let the tomatoes cool*** on the baking sheet pan for 15 minutes or so. Transfer the tomatoes (and all their juices) to the bowl of a food processor. Process, pulsing repeatedly, until a sauce forms. It will be a rough sauce but should be more smooth than chunky. It will have a rosy, almost brick-red color and be very flavorful. Taste and season the sauce with a tiny bit more salt or vinegar, if you like. (If using the sauce for pizza, don't overseason, as the cheese on the pizza will contribute salt. If using the sauce for pasta, season a bit more boldly.)

6 ***Store the sauce*** in a covered container in the fridge for up to 3 days and in the freezer for up to 6 weeks.

Pizza Margherita

with Homemade Sauce, Fresh Mozzarella & Fresh Herbs

{Baked Pizzas} Forget boring! There's a simple and delicious brilliance to a classic pizza Margherita. It's all about the red, the white, and the green. (Yes, the colors of the Italian flag.) The white and green parts are easy: Fresh mozzarella and fresh basil are two ingredients you can put your hands on. But a good red sauce for pizza? Not so easy. If you happen to find a store-bought one you like, go for it, especially if you're short on time. But if you really want to enjoy this perfect marriage of cheese, sauce, and crust, try making a sauce like my tasty purée of quick-roasted plum tomatoes. As good as a simple Margherita is, it also happens to make a nice base for a few extra veggies. My favorites are roasted eggplant (see Roasted Eggplant Slices, page 179) and sautéed mushrooms.

This recipe includes enough topping ingredients for four pizzas. If you're only making one of these pizzas, divide all the topping ingredients by four before prepping. If you're making all four of these pizzas, you might want to divide the topping ingredients into quarters before you start, so you won't have to eyeball as you assemble.

MAKES 4 INDIVIDUAL PIZZAS

2 tsp chopped GARLIC

2 tbsp EXTRA-VIRGIN OLIVE OIL, plus more for drizzling

2 tsp coarsely chopped FRESH OREGANO

2 tsp coarsely chopped FRESH THYME

1 cup/240 ml QUICK-ROASTED PLUM TOMATO PIZZA SAUCE (page 167)

½ lb/225 g FRESH MOZZARELLA, thinly sliced (halved or quartered first, if large ball)

¾ cup/85 g coarsely grated PARMIGIANO-REGGIANO (I use a food processor; see page 212.)

⅓ cup/10 g thinly sliced or torn FRESH BASIL

KOSHER SALT

CORNMEAL for the pizza peel or baking sheet

FLOUR for dusting

Four 7½-oz/215-g balls EASY FOOD-PROCESSOR PIZZA DOUGH (page 164), risen

1 ***Put a baking stone*** on the lowest rack of your oven and preheat the oven to 500°F/260°C/gas 10.

2 ***In a small bowl,*** combine the garlic and the 2 tbsp olive oil. In another small bowl, combine the oregano and thyme. Arrange the garlic oil, the pizza sauce, the cheeses, the herbs, the olive oil for drizzling, and salt around your work area.

3 ***Sprinkle a pizza peel*** or the back of a large baking sheet with cornmeal. Lightly flour a work surface, your hands, and a rolling pin. Gently press one dough ball out with your fingers and hands until it forms a flat cake. Using the rolling pin, roll the dough out to a 9-in/23-cm round. If the dough is bouncy, let it rest between rolls. Transfer the rolled dough to the pizza peel or baking sheet.

4 ***Spoon a quarter of the garlic oil*** onto the dough and brush it or use the back of a spoon to spread it all over the dough, leaving a 3/4-in/2-cm border around the edge. Spoon a scant 1/4 cup/60 ml of the pizza sauce onto the dough and spread it around with the back of a spoon, again leaving a 3/4-in/2-cm border around the edge. Distribute one-quarter of the mozzarella slices evenly over the pizza. Sprinkle one-quarter (about 1 tsp) of the mixed herbs and one-quarter (about 3 tbsp) of the Parmigiano over the pizza. Drizzle the pizza with a little olive oil and sprinkle it with salt.

5 ***Transfer the pizza to the oven*** and cook until the crust is golden brown around the edges and crisp and golden on the bottom (check with tongs), 8 to 10 minutes. (The dough will be more breadlike at 8 minutes; more crackerlike at 9 or 10 minutes.) Use the peel (or tongs and a baking sheet) to transfer the pizza to a wooden cutting board. Sprinkle one-quarter of the fresh basil over the pizza. Slice and serve right away.

6 ***Repeat with the remaining three balls of dough*** and the remaining ingredients.

Potato Carpaccio Pizza

with Gruyère & Rosemary

2 tsp minced GARLIC

5 tbsp/75 ml EXTRA-VIRGIN OLIVE OIL, plus more for drizzling

1½ lb/680 g YUKON GOLD POTATOES, unpeeled

KOSHER SALT

1 tbsp plus 1 tsp chopped FRESH ROSEMARY

1⅓ cups/115 g grated GRUYÈRE

½ cup/55 g grated FONTINA or packaged grated MOZZARELLA

3 tbsp coarsely grated PARMIGIANO-REGGIANO (I use the food processor; see page 212.)

CORNMEAL for the pizza peel or baking sheet

FLOUR for dusting

Four 7½-oz/215-g balls EASY FOOD-PROCESSOR PIZZA DOUGH (page 164), risen

{Baked Pizzas} I always wanted to make a potato pizza but wondered whether to cook the potatoes first before using them on a pizza. Finally, I tried both ways, and found that no precooking was necessary—yay! Thinly sliced raw Yukon golds cook through perfectly on top of the pizza in the 500°F/260°C heat, and they taste great, too, especially with a little garlic oil, some nutty Gruyère cheese, and a sprinkling of rosemary. To make the best version of this pizza, roll the crust to a full 10 in/25 cm (it will be thin and crispy) and slice the potatoes as thinly as you can. Use a thin-bladed knife, like a *santoku*; you don't need a mandoline. Once the potatoes are seasoned with salt, they begin to weep water, so prep them just before assembling. If there'll be long lapses between pizzas, season only one-quarter of the potatoes at a time.

This recipe makes enough topping ingredients for four pizzas. If you're only making one of these pizzas, divide all the topping ingredients by 4 before prepping. If you're making all four of these pizzas, you might want to divide the topping ingredients into quarters before you start, so you won't have to eyeball as you assemble.

MAKES 4 INDIVIDUAL PIZZAS

1 ***Put a baking stone*** on the lowest rack of your oven and preheat the oven to 500°F/260°C/gas 10.

2 ***In a small bowl,*** combine the garlic and 2 tbsp of the olive oil. Halve the potatoes lengthwise. With the potato halves cut-side down, trim the ends and cut the halves crosswise as thinly as possible. (Don't worry about even slices; just go for super-thin—some might be half slices.) In a medium bowl, toss the potato slices with 3 tbsp of the olive oil, 1 tsp salt, and 2 tsp of the rosemary. Arrange the garlic oil, the cheeses, rosemary, salt, olive oil for drizzling, and potatoes around your work area.

3 ***Sprinkle a pizza peel*** or the back of a large baking sheet with cornmeal. Lightly flour a work surface, your hands, and a rolling pin. Gently press one dough ball out with your fingers and hands until it forms a flat cake. Using the rolling pin, roll the dough out to a 9-in/23-cm round (or a 10-in/25-cm round for a pizza that's slightly thinner and crispier). If the dough is bouncy, let it rest between rolls. Transfer the rolled dough to the pizza peel or baking sheet.

4 ***Brush one-quarter of the garlic oil over the dough,*** leaving a 3/4-in/2-cm border around the edge. Distribute 2 tbsp of the Fontina and about 1/3 cup/35 g of the Gruyère evenly over the dough, again leaving a 3/4-in/2-cm border. Arrange one-quarter of the potato slices over the cheese, very slightly overlapping in a concentric pattern. (I start by making a ring around the outside edge and then another toward the center, and so on.) Sprinkle with a little salt, a little more rosemary, and one-quarter of the Parmigiano. Drizzle with a tiny bit more olive oil.

5 ***Transfer the pizza to the oven*** and cook until the crust is golden brown around the edges and crisp and golden on the bottom (check with tongs), 8 to 10 minutes. (The dough will be more breadlike at 8 minutes, more crackerlike at 9 or 10 minutes.) Use the peel (or tongs and a baking sheet) to transfer the pizza to a wooden cutting board. Slice and serve right away.

6 ***Repeat with the remaining three balls of dough*** and the remaining ingredients

Broccoli Raab, Sausage, Goat Cheese & Sun-Dried Tomato Pizza

{Baked Pizzas} This pizza is my hands-down favorite way to introduce people to broccoli raab, because all the flavors bring out the best in this bitter green. I've always loved ordering broccoli raab pizza in traditional Italian restaurants, so I wanted to re-create one at home. I realized right away that the raab would need its classic seasoning of garlic, crushed red pepper, and a little lemon, and that the tart creaminess of goat cheese would soothe it, too. And I decided to go for a little meat on this pizza, since sausage is such a tasty partner for raab, too. Raab is packed with good stuff (vitamins A and C), so I didn't want anyone to miss out on this. Turns out my greens-averse friends loved it.

This recipe includes enough topping ingredients for four pizzas. If you're only making one of these pizzas, divide all the topping ingredients by 4 before prepping. If you're making all four of these pizzas, you might want to divide the topping ingredients into quarters before you start, so you won't have to eyeball as you assemble.

MAKES 4 INDIVIDUAL PIZZAS

KOSHER SALT

12 oz/340 g BROCCOLI RAAB (with tough lower stems or thick stems trimmed before weighing)

⅓ cup/75 ml EXTRA-VIRGIN OLIVE OIL, plus more for drizzling

1 tbsp plus 1 tsp minced GARLIC

½ tsp (packed) finely grated LEMON ZEST

¼ tsp crushed RED PEPPER FLAKES

½ cup/55 g coarsely grated PARMIGIANO-REGGIANO (I use a food processor; see page 212.)

4 oz/115 g cold FRESH GOAT CHEESE, crumbled while still chilled

½ cup/75 g sliced OIL-PACKED SUN-DRIED TOMATOES (no need to pat dry)

½ lb/225 g SWEET ITALIAN SAUSAGE PATTIES (or meat from links with casing removed), torn into small pieces and cooked until all trace of pink is gone

CORNMEAL for the pizza peel or baking sheet

FLOUR for dusting

Four 7½-oz/215-g balls of EASY FOOD-PROCESSOR PIZZA DOUGH (page 164), risen

1 ***Put a baking stone*** on the lowest rack of your oven and preheat the oven to 500°F/260°C/gas 10.

2 ***Bring a pot of water to a boil*** and add ½ tsp salt. Drop in the broccoli raab and cook, uncovered, for 4 minutes. (It will still be bright green but tender to the bite.) Drain immediately in a colander and briefly run under cold water to begin cooling. Let sit until cool enough to handle, then wrap the raab in paper towels or a dish towel and gently squeeze any excess water out without crushing the vegetable. Chop into ½-in/12-mm pieces and set aside.

3 ***In a small bowl,*** combine the olive oil, garlic, lemon zest, and red pepper flakes. Stir or whisk to thoroughly combine. Arrange the garlic oil, the cheeses, sun-dried tomatoes, raab, salt, and olive oil for drizzling near your work area.

4 ***Sprinkle a pizza peel*** or the back of a large baking sheet with cornmeal. Lightly flour a work surface, your hands, and a rolling pin. Gently press one dough ball out with your fingers and hands until it forms a flat cake. Using the rolling pin, roll the dough out to a 9-in/23-cm round. If the dough is bouncy, let it rest between rolls. Transfer the rolled dough to the pizza peel or baking sheet.

5 ***Brush the dough*** with 1 tbsp of the garlic oil, leaving a ¾-in/2-cm border around the edge. Sprinkle 1 tbsp of the Parmigiano over the dough, again leaving a ¾-in/2-cm border. Arrange one-quarter of the sun-dried tomatoes, one-quarter of the goat cheese, one-quarter of the raab, and one-quarter of the sausage over the Parmigiano. (Put the sun-dried tomatoes on first, as they benefit from being covered up a bit.) Spoon or drizzle 1 tsp of the garlic oil over the toppings. Sprinkle with a little salt and the remaining 1 tbsp Parmigiano and drizzle with a little bit of the olive oil.

6 ***Transfer the pizza to the oven*** and cook until the crust is golden brown around the edges and crisp and golden on the bottom (check with tongs), 8 to 10 minutes. (The dough will be more breadlike at 8 minutes, more crackerlike at 9 or 10 minutes.) Use the peel (or tongs and a baking sheet) to transfer the pizza to a wooden cutting board. Slice and serve right away.

7 ***Repeat with the remaining three balls of dough*** and the remaining ingredients.

Roasted Eggplant Slices

3 tbsp EXTRA-VIRGIN OLIVE OIL, plus more for parchment

1 small EGGPLANT (about ½ lb/ 225 g), such as Italian eggplant or small globe eggplant

KOSHER SALT

These slices of roasted eggplant are really versatile: great on pizza, yes, but great for baked pastas, in gratins, or on top of Grilled Bread (page 203), too. So don't worry if you have extras. This recipe will yield enough slices for two to three baked pizzas or one to two grilled pizzas (see Pizza Margherita, page 169, or Summer-on-a-Pizza, page 181). I usually don't flip the slices halfway through cooking, as I don't mind the bottom side being browner. But if you want to flip, use a thin spatula and be careful; the slices are delicate.

MAKES 14 TO 16 SLICES

Heat the oven to 450°F/230°C/gas 8. Line a heavy-duty baking sheet with parchment. Brush the paper with olive oil. Score the skin of the eggplant with a fork, trim the ends, and halve lengthwise. Cut each half crosswise into 3/8- to 1/2-in-/1-cm- to 12-mm-thick half-moon slices. Arrange the slices in a single layer on the baking sheet and, using a pastry brush, brush both sides of each slice with the 3 tbsp olive oil. Season the tops with a scant 1/4 tsp salt and roast, carefully flipping once halfway through cooking (if desired), until the eggplant is tender and lightly browned, 20 to 22 minutes. (The undersides will be slightly browner, and the slices will be somewhat shrunken.)

Garlic Oil

4 tbsp/60 ml EXTRA-VIRGIN OLIVE OIL

1 tbsp plus 1 tsp minced GARLIC

If you only want to make garlic oil for one pizza, divide this recipe by 4.

MAKES ENOUGH FOR 4 PIZZAS

In a small bowl, combine the olive oil and garlic and stir. Let sit for a few minutes to infuse. Cover tightly with plastic wrap and refrigerate if not using right away. Do not keep for more than 24 hours.

Summer-on-a-Pizza

with Corn, Tomatoes & Arugula

EXTRA-VIRGIN OLIVE OIL

One 7½-oz/215-g ball EASY FOOD-PROCESSOR PIZZA DOUGH (page 164), risen

1 tbsp GARLIC OIL (page 179)

3 tbsp coarsely grated PARMIGIANO-REGGIANO (I use the food processor; see page 212.)

10 to 12 ROASTED EGGPLANT SLICES (page 179)

⅓ cup/40 g FRESH CORN KERNELS, cut from about ½ small ear, blanched (see page 213)

¼ cup/40 g diced or sliced OIL-PACKED SUN-DRIED TOMATOES, drained, or ⅓ cup/55 g cup ROASTED CHERRY TOMATOES (page 91)

⅓ cup/40 g cold FRESH GOAT CHEESE, crumbled while still cold

KOSHER SALT

15 to 20 small WHOLE MINT LEAVES or torn bigger leaves or 1 tbsp finely sliced MINT LEAVES

½ to ¾ oz/15 to 20 g (1 cup loosely packed) BABY ARUGULA LEAVES

{Grilled Pizzas} This pizza has all my favorite late-summer veggies on it, including fresh corn, tomatoes, eggplant, and even arugula. While I like to use Roasted Cherry Tomatoes, the pizza is equally delicious with sun-dried tomatoes. My method for roasting eggplant slices couldn't be easier, and blanching corn is quick, but you'll have to plan ahead to cook these things. The rest of the topping comes together easily. I love garnishing this pizza with a shower of baby arugula leaves. I don't usually dress them, but you could toss them with a bit of lemon and olive oil, if you like. Don't skip the mint; it's a great partner for arugula and the rest of the pizza.

MAKES 1 INDIVIDUAL PIZZA

1 ***Heat a gas grill*** by turning all burners to medium-high for at least 15 minutes.

2 ***Before grilling the pizza,*** lower one burner to low heat. (If your grill has two burners—most likely on the right and left as you face the grill—turn either one down. If your grill has three burners—most likely arranged back to front—turn the front burner down.) If your grill runs very hot, you might want to turn the medium-high burner down to medium at this point.

3 ***In the kitchen or outside near the grill,*** invert a sheet pan and brush or rub it generously with olive oil. Take the dough, plop it on the sheet pan, and spread it out with your fingers and hands into a thin free-form shape about 10 in/25 cm in diameter and ⅛ to ¼ in/3 to 6 mm thick. (I find that a square shape works better than a circle; it stretches to a rectangle or oblong by the time you get it on the grill and will then fit over your low burner (if it's a narrow one) when you go to top it. But you will find through trial and error what shape works for you.)

4 ***Using two hands,*** pick up two corners of the dough (the two corners farthest away from you) like a hanky and gently but quickly drape it over the hotter burners, letting the bottom edges touch down first so that you can lay the rest of the dough evenly over the grates. The dough will lengthen and stretch out during the time it takes you to get it on the grill. That's okay; thin is good. And don't worry if you have a very thin spot or a hole. The dough will immediately begin to puff. Cover the grill and cook for 2 to 2½ minutes.

→

5 ***Using tongs,*** check the underside of the dough. It should be marked with grill marks and be very lightly browned all over. If not, cover the grill again and cook for 1 minute more. Uncover and check again. If it looks good, flip the dough over. (Don't forget this flipping step. The browned side should now be up! That is the side you want to put the toppings on.) Move the dough to the cooler part of the grill to add your toppings. (Alternatively, you can pull the flipped dough off the grill onto an oiled baking sheet, close the grill to keep the heat in, and top your pizza off the grill.)

6 ***Brush the top of the dough*** generously with the garlic oil. You can also use the back of a spoon to spread it all over the crust.

7 ***Sprinkle the dough*** with 2 tbsp of the Parmigiano. Distribute the eggplant slices, corn kernels, tomatoes, and goat cheese over the dough. Sprinkle with the remaining 1 tbsp Parmigiano and a little kosher salt. Drizzle with a little olive oil.

8 ***Using tongs,*** transfer the topped pizza back to the hottest part of the grill. Cover and cook until the underside is browned and marked and the toppings are warmed through (the cheeses should be somewhat melted), another 2 to 3 minutes. Check frequently. If at any time the bottom of the pizza is getting too brown, move it back over to the cooler part of the grill and re-cover to let the toppings finish heating. Or if the pizza is cooking faster at one end, use the tongs to maneuver the pizza around so that the areas that need the most heat get it. (You can also reduce the heat slightly on the hotter burners.)

9 ***Bring a cutting board right to the grill,*** and using tongs, pull the cooked pizza directly onto the board. Top with the mint and arugula. Let cool for 1 or 2 minutes and cut into as many pieces as you like with a wide-wheel pizza cutter or a chef's knife. (With oblong shapes I find it easiest to cut the pizza into 2- to 3-in-/5- to 7.5-cm-wide strips and then in half to form square or rectangular pieces.) Serve right away.

Walk-in-the-Woods Grilled Pizza

2 tbsp GARLIC OIL (page 179)

1 tbsp SOY SAUCE

2 tsp ASIAN SESAME OIL

1 tbsp RICE WINE

EXTRA-VIRGIN OLIVE OIL

12 large FRESH SHIITAKE MUSHROOMS, stemmed

8 medium CREMINI or BABY BELLA MUSHROOMS, stemmed

One 7½-oz/215-g ball EASY FOOD-PROCESSOR PIZZA DOUGH (page 164), risen

⅓ cup/40 g coarsely grated FONTINA

3 tbsp coarsely grated GRUYÈRE

1 tsp chopped FRESH SAGE

KOSHER SALT

PURE MAPLE SYRUP for drizzling

{Grilled Pizzas} There's nothing like using the intense woodsy flavor of grilled marinated mushrooms for a pizza topping, and a drizzle of maple syrup at the end contrasts the smoky and herby flavors. Marinate and grill the mushrooms before you make your pizza, but you can do the rest of the prep while your dough is proofing.

MAKES 1 INDIVIDUAL PIZZA

1 ***In a medium mixing bowl,*** whisk together 1 tbsp of the garlic oil, the soy sauce, sesame oil, rice wine, and 2 tbsp extra-virgin olive oil. Add the shiitake and cremini mushrooms to the marinade and toss well. Let sit for at least 15 minutes or up to 30 minutes, stirring occasionally.

2 ***Heat a gas grill to medium for 15 minutes.*** Put all the mushroom caps, stem-side up, on the grill grates. Cook the shiitake mushrooms until they are well marked on the bottom, about 2 minutes. Flip them and cook them until the other side is marked, about 2 minutes more. Cook the cremini until they are well marked on the cap side, 3 to 4 minutes. Turn them over (they will have liquid pooled in them) and cook until the other side is marked and the mushrooms are softened and cooked through (the inside of the mushroom will look grey, not white), another 3 to 4 minutes. Transfer the mushrooms to a cutting board to cool slightly. Cut into thin slices.

3 ***Before grilling the pizza,*** lower one burner to low heat. (If your grill has two burners—most likely on the right and left as you face the grill—turn either one down. If your grill has three burners—most likely arranged back to front—turn the front burner down.) If your grill runs very hot, you might want to turn the medium-high burner down to medium at this point.

4 ***In the kitchen or outside near the grill,*** invert a sheet pan and brush or rub it generously with olive oil. Take the dough, plop it on the sheet pan, and spread it out with your fingers and hands into a thin free-form shape about 10 in/25 cm in diameter and ⅛ to ¼ in/3 to 6 mm thick. (I find that a square shape works better than a circle; it stretches to a rectangle or oblong by the time you get it on the grill and will then fit over your low burner (if it's a narrow one) when you go to top it. But you will find through trial and error what shape works for you.)

5 ***Using two hands,*** pick up two corners of the dough (the two corners farthest away from you) like a hanky and gently but quickly drape it over the hotter burners, letting the bottom edges touch down first so that you can lay the rest of the dough evenly over the grates. The dough will lengthen and stretch out during the time it takes you to get it on the grill. That's okay; thin is good. And don't worry if you have a very thin spot or a hole. The dough will immediately begin to puff. Cover the grill and cook for 2 to 2½ minutes.

6 ***Using tongs,*** check the underside of the dough. It should be marked with grill marks and be very lightly browned all over. If not, cover the grill again and cook for 1 minute more. Uncover and check again. If it looks good, flip the dough over. (Don't forget this flipping step. The browned side should now be up! That is the side you want to put the toppings on.) Move the dough to the cooler part of the grill to add your toppings. (Alternatively, you can pull the flipped dough off the grill onto an oiled baking sheet, close the grill to keep the heat in, and top your pizza off the grill.)

7 ***Brush the top of the dough*** generously with the garlic oil. You can also use the back of a spoon to spread it all over the crust.

8 ***Sprinkle the dough with the Fontina.*** Distribute the sliced mushrooms over the Fontina and sprinkle with the Gruyère. Sprinkle evenly with the sage and a little salt. Drizzle with olive oil.

9 ***Using tongs,*** transfer the topped pizza back to the hottest part of the grill. Cover and cook until the underside is browned and marked and the toppings are warmed through (the cheeses should be somewhat melted), another 2 to 3 minutes. Check frequently. If at any time the bottom of the pizza is getting too brown, move it back over to the cooler part of the grill and re-cover to let the toppings finish heating. Or if the pizza is cooking faster at one end, use the tongs to maneuver the pizza around so that the areas that need the most heat get it. (You can also reduce the heat slightly on the hotter burners.)

10 ***Bring a cutting board right to the grill,*** and using tongs, pull the cooked pizza directly onto the board. Drizzle with maple syrup. Let cool for 1 or 2 minutes and cut into as many pieces as you like with a wide-wheel pizza cutter or a chef's knife. (With oblong shapes I find it easiest to cut the pizza into 2- to 3-in-/5- to 7.5-cm-wide strips and then in half to form square or rectangular pieces.) Serve right away.

Sicilian Fig, Gorgonzola & Sweet Onion Grilled Pizza

½ tbsp UNSALTED BUTTER

2 tbsp plus 1 tsp EXTRA-VIRGIN OLIVE OIL, plus more for drizzling

1 small sweet ONION (about 9 oz/255 g), such as Vidalia, cut crosswise into 3/8-in-/1-cm-wide rings

KOSHER SALT

1 tsp ORANGE JUICE

1 tsp BALSAMIC VINEGAR

1 tsp HONEY, plus more for drizzling

1½ oz/40 g DRIED CALIFORNIA MISSION FIGS (I like Sunmaid), stemmed and cut crosswise into thin slices (¼ to ⅓ cup)

One 7½-oz/215-g ball EASY FOOD-PROCESSOR PIZZA DOUGH (page 164), risen

3 tbsp coarsely grated PARMIGIANO-REGGIANO

⅓ cup/40 g cold SWEET GORGONZOLA (best quality you can find), crumbled while cold

2 tsp chopped FRESH ROSEMARY

{Grilled Pizzas} This lovely combination of toppings comes together in less than 15 minutes. You'll need a good blue cheese, like a sweet Gorgonzola or Roquefort; the chalky, precrumbled stuff can be overly salty and will ruin your pizza. Sunmaid figs are easy to find at the grocery packed in foil bags, and are still relatively moist. If your figs are drier, soak them in a marinade for a few minutes. If you have fresh figs, by all means, use them. Be sure to add the drizzle of honey at the end; it really brings all the flavors together.

MAKES 1 INDIVIDUAL PIZZA

1 ***In a medium heavy nonstick skillet,*** heat the butter and 1 tbsp of the olive oil over medium heat. Add the onion and ¼ tsp salt and stir. Cover and cook until softened and somewhat limp, about 5 minutes. Uncover, lower the heat to medium-low, and cook until lightly golden, another 12 to 15 minutes. Transfer the onion to a plate to cool.

2 ***In a small bowl,*** whisk together the orange juice, vinegar, honey, and 1 tsp of the olive oil until well combined. Add the figs, stir, and let sit, stirring occasionally, until ready to grill.

3 ***Heat a gas grill*** by turning all burners to medium-high for at least 15 minutes.

4 ***Before grilling the pizza,*** lower one burner to low heat. (If your grill has two burners—most likely on the right and left as you face the grill—turn either one down. If your grill has three burners—most likely arranged back to front—turn the front burner down.) If your grill runs very hot, you might want to turn the medium-high burner down to medium at this point.

5 ***In the kitchen or outside near the grill,*** invert a sheet pan and brush or rub it generously with olive oil. Take the dough, plop it on the sheet pan, and spread it out with your fingers and hands into a thin free-form shape about 10 in/25 cm in diameter and 1/8 to 1/4 in/3 to 6 mm thick. (I find that a square shape works better than a circle; it stretches to a rectangle or oblong by the time you get it on the grill and will then fit over your low burner (if it's a narrow one) when you go to top it. But you will find through trial and error what shape works for you.)

6 ***Using two hands,*** pick up two corners of the dough (the two corners farthest away from you) like a hanky and gently but quickly drape it over the hotter burners, letting the bottom edges touch down first so that you can lay the rest of the dough evenly over the grates. The dough will lengthen and stretch out during the time it takes you to get it on the grill. That's okay; thin is good. And don't worry if you have a very thin spot or a hole. The dough will immediately begin to puff. Cover the grill and cook for 2 to 2½ minutes.

7 ***Using tongs,*** check the underside of the dough. It should be marked with grill marks and be very lightly browned all over. If not, cover the grill again and cook for 1 minute more. Uncover and check again. If it looks good, flip the dough over. (Don't forget this flipping step. The browned side should now be up! That is the side you want to put the toppings on.) Move the dough to the cooler part of the grill to add your toppings. (Alternatively, you can pull the flipped dough off the grill onto an oiled baking sheet, close the grill to keep the heat in, and top your pizza off the grill.)

8 ***Brush the top of the dough*** generously with the garlic oil. You can also use the back of a spoon to spread it all over the crust.

9 ***Sprinkle the dough*** with 2 tbsp of the Parmigiano. Distribute the onion, figs (leaving any marinade behind), and the blue cheese over the pizza and sprinkle with 1 tsp of the rosemary, the remaining 1 tbsp Parmigiano, and a little salt. Drizzle with a little olive oil and a nice bit of honey.

10 ***Using tongs,*** transfer the topped pizza back to the hottest part of the grill. Cover and cook until the underside is browned and marked and the toppings are warmed through (the cheeses should be somewhat melted), another 2 to 3 minutes. Check frequently. If at any time the bottom of the pizza is getting too brown, move it back over to the cooler part of the grill and re-cover to let the toppings finish heating. Or if the pizza is cooking faster at one end, use the tongs to maneuver the pizza around so that the areas that need the most heat get it. (You can also reduce the heat slightly on the hotter burners.)

11 ***Bring a cutting board right to the grill,*** and using tongs, pull the cooked pizza directly onto the board. Top with the remaining 1 tsp rosemary. Let cool for 1 or 2 minutes and cut into as many pieces as you like with a wide-wheel pizza cutter or a chef's knife. (With oblong shapes I find it easiest to cut the pizza into 2- to 3-in-/5- to 7.5-cm-wide strips and then in half to form square or rectangular pieces.) Serve right away.

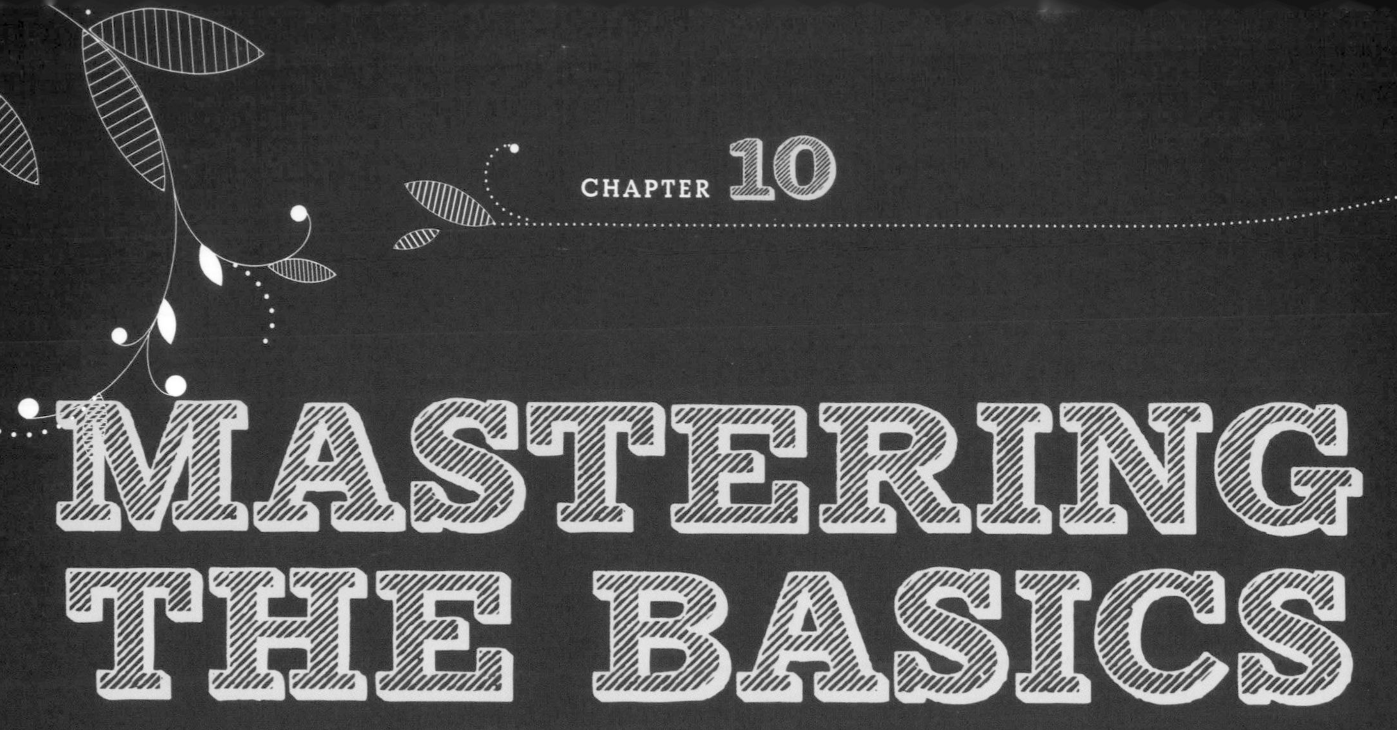

TIPS, TECHNIQUES & RECIPES TO PUMP UP THE FLAVOR IN THE VEGGIE KITCHEN

Mastering the Basics: How It Works

It's the little stuff that counts. When it comes to the veggie main-dish kitchen, this couldn't be more true. There are dozens of tiny tricks and tips you can use to dial up the flavor and even improve texture in your recipes. Some of these—like toasting nuts or grinding Parmigiano in a food processor—work within the context of the recipe you're making. Others—like grilled bread, crunchy croutons, creamy polenta, or a basic white-rice pilaf—add another dimension to a recipe, a finishing touch that makes the main dish a whole meal. And then there are essential tips—like how to slice a wobbly vegetable that just make life in the veggie kitchen easier. In this chapter, I've highlighted the five areas where most of these tips, tricks—and even recipes—hang out. I hope you'll find them helpful and use them often to make great meals that feature veggie main dishes.

How to Make a Great Green Salad

Here goes Susie's mini manifesto on greens. I am incredibly picky about fresh greens, probably because I once had a restaurant boss who told me I'd be fired on the spot if I ever sent a salad to the dining room with wilted lettuce in it. (Also, I grow a lot of greens and value that fresh factor immensely.) At the same time, I'm also super-aware of the time drain that preparing a green salad can be. But I've found that with just a little planning—and a very small investment of extra time, I can make my own salad mixes and vinaigrettes and wind up with far superior salads and less waste. The problem with packaged salad mixes is that they're often old before you get them home, and they go bad quickly. Plus, many of them feature tender lettuces, which don't hold up well with warm ingredients. And bottled salad dressings harbor all kinds of things you don't need to ingest. For crisp, fresh, delicious salads, follow these tips.

1 ***Make your own custom mix of greens:*** Buy one great head of lettuce—sturdy escarole or frisée in winter, silky Bibb or crisp romaine in summer. Mix in your choice of dark green baby leaves; arugula, mizuna, spinach, and tatsoi will all work. Last, add a little contrast with a bit of thinly sliced radicchio, endive, napa cabbage, or even fennel. Your trio is your custom mix.

2 ***Wash greens as soon as you get home.*** Separate the leaves from the heads of lettuce (prewashed baby green leaves like arugula can stay in packaging), submerge the leaves in a bowl of tepid (not cold) water, and swish the leaves around. Let them sit for a few minutes and then gently lift them out. Dump the water and rinse out the silt that will have settled at the bottom of the bowl. If the lettuce was very dirty, do this once more with tepid water. Otherwise, now submerge the lettuce in cold water and let it sit and crisp up for a few minutes.

Drain, spin dry, and pack the leaves loosely in paper towel– (or dish towel–) lined zip-top bags. The lettuce will stay crisp and fresh for most of the week. All you have to do come dinnertime is pull out a few leaves, toss in a handful of the baby arugula, and

FOR THE DRESSING

3 tbsp EXTRA-VIRGIN OLIVE OIL

1 tbsp plus 1½ tsp freshly squeezed LIME JUICE

¼ tsp LIME ZEST

1 tsp HONEY

½ tsp minced GARLIC

1 tsp WHITE BALSAMIC VINEGAR

KOSHER SALT

FRESHLY GROUND PEPPER

FOR THE SALAD

2 heads BIBB, or 1 small head BOSTON LETTUCE largest outer leaves and damaged leaves removed, torn into bite-size pieces (about 3½ cups)

2 small BELGIAN ENDIVE, damaged leaves removed, cored, and thinly sliced (about 3 cups)

1½ cups/30 g BABY ARUGULA LEAVES

¼ cup/6 g loosely packed FRESH PARSLEY

KOSHER SALT

1 small ripe but firm AVOCADO

12 colorful small CHERRY TOMATOES or GRAPE TOMATOES, halved if very small, quartered if larger

2 RADISHES, halved and thinly sliced

2 SCALLIONS (white and light green parts), cut on the diagonal into very thin slices

1 ***To make the dressing:*** In a small bowl or glass jar, combine the olive oil, lime juice, lime zest, honey, garlic, vinegar, a big pinch of salt, and a few grinds of fresh pepper. Whisk together or shake well.

2 ***To make the salad:*** Arrange four salad plates on your counter. In a shallow mixing bowl, combine the lettuce, endive, arugula, and parsley. Sprinkle very lightly with salt. Drizzle 2 tbsp of the dressing over the greens and toss gently. Divide the greens evenly among the four salad plates.

3 ***Halve the avocado and remove the pit.*** Slide a large spoon between the skin and flesh to peel each half. Turn the avocado halves cut-side down and cut them into small or medium dice. Put the avocado in a small bowl, put the cherry tomato halves in another small bowl, and combine the radishes and scallions in a third small bowl. Drizzle the avocados with 2 tsp of the dressing, the tomatoes with 1 tsp, and the scallions and radishes with 1 tsp. Gently toss each mixture.

4 ***Divide the avocado pieces*** and the cherry tomato halves evenly among the four salad plates, tucking them in among the greens. Sprinkle the radishes and scallions over each salad. If you have a little bit of dressing left, drizzle it over the four salads. Serve right away.

Winter Green & White Side Salad

with Blue Cheese & Hazelnuts

In wintertime, I love to use "white" greens like endive and the lovely yellowish-white inner leaves of escarole. Paired with dark green baby arugula, these make a handsome salad and one that's classically crisp and bright, too. It's the perfect refreshing counterpart to hearty gratins and ragoûts. Here, I've paired the greens with my favorite sherry-maple vinaigrette and added a creamy, savory element with a good blue cheese. (Avoid tasteless "crumbles" and choose creamy Roquefort or tangy Stilton.) I finish the salad with toasted hazelnuts. If you can, buy hazelnuts that have already been skinned. (Find them, chopped, in the baking aisle of groceries, or buy them whole and skinned at natural-foods stores.) You can prep the greens ahead and refrigerate them in the salad bowl, covered with a damp cloth. Make the vinaigrette up to a week ahead. To serve a crowd, you'll need to double only the salad ingredients; there's plenty of vinaigrette in one batch.

SERVES 4

FOR THE VINAIGRETTE

7 tbsp/105 ml EXTRA-VIRGIN OLIVE OIL

2 tbsp SHERRY VINEGAR

1 tsp ORANGE JUICE

1 tsp PURE MAPLE SYRUP

½ tsp finely grated LEMON ZEST

½ tsp DIJON MUSTARD

KOSHER SALT

FRESHLY GROUND PEPPER

FOR THE SALAD

3 oz/85 g BABY ARUGULA LEAVES (about 6 cups, loosely packed)

3 oz/85 g INNER ESCAROLE LEAVES (white, yellow, and palest green parts), torn into small pieces (about 4 cups)

2 small BELGIAN ENDIVE, cut crosswise into ¾-in-/2-cm-wide pieces and core discarded (about 2½ cups)

½ cup/85 g ROQUEFORT, STILTON, or OTHER GOOD-QUALITY BLUE CHEESE, crumbled while still cold

½ cup/50 g very coarsely chopped TOASTED HAZELNUTS, (see page 198)

1 *To make the vinaigrette:* In a glass jar or liquid measuring cup, combine the olive oil, vinegar, orange juice, maple syrup, lemon zest, mustard, about ⅛ tsp salt, and several grinds of pepper. Whisk together or shake well.

2 *To make the salad:* Put the arugula, escarole, and endive in a wide shallow bowl and toss with your hands to combine. Spoon 2 to 3 tbsp of the vinaigrette over the leaves and toss well. Taste and add just a bit more dressing, if needed. Add the blue cheese to the salad and gently mix it with the greens (again using your hands), breaking the blue cheese up further to distribute it throughout the greens. (A creamy blue will smear slightly, which is a good thing.)

3 *Divide the salad evenly among four plates,* mounding it in the center, and sprinkle the toasted hazelnuts over each. Serve right away.

Simple Lemony Arugula Salad

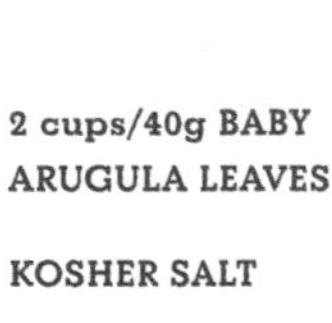

- 2 cups/40g BABY ARUGULA LEAVES
- KOSHER SALT
- 2 tsp EXTRA-VIRGIN OLIVE OIL
- 1/4 large LEMON

Sometimes a simple little salad is all you need to dress up a pizza, a piece of grilled bread, a veggie galette—or any number of dishes. Something about the color and height and bright flavor of a delicate mound of greens can just make a dish look—and taste—finished. For a super-quick fix, I pair baby arugula leaves with lemon (a natural flavor partner), olive oil, and salt. This lively combo makes a great contrast for the earthy eggplant galette on page 113, but it could work with a potato galette (page 111) or with a white pizza (page 172) too.

SERVES 2 TO 4

Put the arugula leaves in a small mixing bowl, sprinkle them with a little salt, and drizzle lightly with the olive oil. Squeeze the lemon lightly over the greens and toss gently. Taste and add more lemon if you like. Serve right away.

How to Make a Crunchy, Toasty (or Nutty!) Garnish

Who doesn't like a little crunch? I've never met a soup or a salad—or for that matter any vegetable dish with silky or soft textures—that doesn't benefit from a little contrast. Could be just a garnish, like croutons or toasted nuts; could be something more substantial, like grilled bread or crostini. Any of these can be the thing that elevates a good dish to a great one, while at the same time adding substance and texture. Most important, homemade versions of these crunchy wonders are so much better than their store-bought kin.

Toast nuts for the best flavor: You can toast whole nuts (especially smaller ones, like pine nuts), but I like to coarsely chop bigger nuts first. I try not to go crazy. I cut each nut into just about three or four pieces. Heat your oven to 375°F/190°C/gas 5. Spread the nuts in one loose single layer on a rimmed, heavy-duty baking sheet. Set your timer to 5 minutes if you like, but don't go far. Most nuts will get to the perfect state of deep golden brown in 7 to 10 minutes. Your biggest clue is smell. When you begin to sniff that nice nutty aroma, check on the nuts. They may need to go a little longer for the best flavor, but don't push it. Golden caramel color is good; dark brown can be bitter. Keep a supply of toasted nuts in the fridge or freezer for an easy supply of garnishes. (Keep most raw nuts—especially walnuts, hazelnuts, and pine nuts—in the freezer. They can go rancid in just a few weeks.)

Make homemade croutons and crostini: In addition to homemade bread crumbs (page 212), croutons and crostini (little toasts) are great destinations for bits of bread. I make both of these crunchy garnishes in the oven and keep extras (that don't get gobbled) in the freezer.

Rustic Croutons

4 oz/115 g BAGUETTE or other crusty bread (including crusts), cut into ¾-in/2-cm cubes

2 tbsp UNSALTED BUTTER

1 tbsp EXTRA-VIRGIN OLIVE OIL

1 large GARLIC CLOVE, smashed and peeled

KOSHER SALT

1 tsp chopped FRESH ROSEMARY or THYME (optional)

2 to 3 tbsp grated PARMIGIANO-REGGIANO or CHEDDAR (optional)

Boxed croutons (hard as rock and overly seasoned) don't stand a chance in our house. Crispy homemade croutons are a world apart. I like big, rustic croutons made from artisan bread for soups and some salads. But you can also use this method to make delicate croutons from smaller-cut English muffins and sandwich bread. Baking time may vary, but the delicious factor prevails.

MAKES ABOUT 2 CUPS

1 ***Preheat the oven to 350°F/180°C/gas 4.*** Line a heavy-duty rimmed baking sheet with parchment. Put the bread cubes in a medium mixing bowl.

2 ***In a small skillet,*** heat the butter and olive oil over low heat. When the butter has melted, add the garlic and break it up further by mashing it with the back of a wooden spoon. Raise the heat to medium and cook until the garlic has just started to turn a light brown around the edges, about 2 minutes. Remove the skillet from the heat and, using a fork, fish out the garlic pieces.

3 ***Drizzle the garlic-infused mixture*** over the bread cubes, stirring with a silicone spatula or wooden spoon as you drizzle. Continue to mix the bread cubes until they are all well coated. Add ¼ tsp salt and the rosemary (if using), and toss well again.

4 ***Arrange the bread cubes*** in a single layer on the prepared baking sheet. (Scrape any remaining salt and herbs out of the bowl onto the bread.) Bake until golden brown, 15 to 17 minutes. If using cheese, bunch the baked croutons close together and sprinkle the cheese over them. Return the baking sheet to the oven and cook until the cheese has melted, about 2 minutes. Let cool completely on the sheet pan.

5 ***The croutons may be stored*** in a heavy zip-top bag in the freezer for up to 1 month.

Crostini

Twelve ½-in-/12-mm-thick slices **BAGUETTE**

2 tbsp **UNSALTED BUTTER**

2 tbsp **OLIVE OIL**

1 large **GARLIC CLOVE**, smashed

KOSHER SALT

Stop! Don't buy those overpriced, overly crisp "crostini" you see in gourmet stores. Make your own. They're easy and keep well in the freezer, so you'll always have them on hand to top with a little something and serve with a soup or salad. These have just the right texture, too: crisp and brown on the top and bottom but soft (not tooth-breaking) on the inside. Try topping them with warm goat cheese, chopped roasted tomatoes, sautéed greens, or caramelized onions.

MAKES 24 CROSTINI

1 ***Position an oven rack*** at the top of the oven, 3 to 4 in/7.5 to 10 cm from the broiler. Preheat the broiler. Line a heavy-duty rimmed sheet pan with parchment or aluminum foil.

2 ***Halve each bread slice*** to make two smaller pieces (about 2 in/5 cm wide) for a total of 24 pieces. Arrange the bread slices in a single layer on the prepared pan.

3 ***In a small skillet,*** heat the butter and olive oil over low heat. When the butter has melted, add the garlic and break it up further by mashing it with the back of a wooden spoon. Raise the heat to medium and cook until the garlic has just started to turn a light brown around the edges, about 2 minutes. Remove the skillet from the heat.

⟶

4 ***Using a pastry brush,*** brush both sides of all the bread pieces with the butter mixture and sprinkle each side with a tiny bit of salt. Put the sheet pan under the broiler and broil until the crostini are lightly browned around the edges and golden in the middle, about 1½ minutes. Keep an eye on the pan and rotate it, if necessary, for even browning. Remove the sheet pan from the oven. Using tongs, turn the crostini over, and, keeping a close eye on the pan, brown the second side, about 45 seconds to 1 minute.

5 ***Let cool on the pan.*** When completely cool, transfer the crostini to a zip-top bag and store in the freezer for up to 3 weeks. To use frozen, let the crostini thaw at room temperature and gently re-crisp in the oven or a toaster oven.

Grilled Bread

Six to eight ½- to ¾-in-/ 12-mm- to 2-cm-thick slices **CRUSTY ARTISAN BREAD**

3 to 4 tbsp **EXTRA-VIRGIN OLIVE OIL**

KOSHER SALT or **COARSE SEA SALT**

1 large **GARLIC CLOVE**, halved and peeled (optional)

Here's your chance to really round out any veggie main dish with a side that's so satisfyingly flavorful and crispy-crunchy that it threatens to steal the show from the veggies. Years ago, every time I made grilled bread, my ninety-year-old father-in-law would ask me, "How do you make that? It tastes so good." And every time, I'd explain to him how simple it was. There's nothing to it really, and yet it's so delicious. There's just no reason not to add it to your repertoire, especially if you're eating a lot of veggies. You can pick up good crusty bread at any grocery store; all you need to do is slice it up. My favorite bread for grilling is ciabatta.

SERVES 3 OR 4

1 ***Heat a gas grill*** to medium.

2 ***Generously brush the bread slices*** on both sides with the olive oil and sprinkle with a little salt. Put the bread directly on the grill grate, cover, and cook until golden brown on both sides, 1 to 2 minutes per side. Rub the bread on one side with the cut sides of the garlic (if using).

3 ***Serve right away.***

3 ***Put the greased popover pan*** in the oven for 3 minutes to preheat. The butter will melt and pool at the bottom of the cups—that's fine. If you forget and leave the pan in a couple of minutes longer, the butter will begin to brown, which is also fine (and tasty). Just don't forget the pan and leave it in there for any longer, or the butter will burn!

4 ***Remove the pan*** from the oven and rest it on a heatproof surface. Divide the batter as evenly as possible among the cups (they will be about three-quarters to seven-eighths full). The butter will sizzle when you pour in the batter—that's good! Quickly return the pan to the oven and do not open the oven door for the entire baking time.

5 ***Bake for 20 minutes*** and then reduce the oven temperature to 325°F/165°C/gas 3. Continue baking (without opening the oven door) until the popovers are very puffed and a deep golden brown, about another 15 minutes.

6 ***Serve right away*** with lots of butter if desired.

TIP: If you don't have a popover pan, you can make smaller, slightly denser (but still delicious) popovers in a nonstick 12-cup muffin pan, dividing the batter evenly among all or most of the cups. Shorten the initial baking time at 425°F/220°C/gas 7 to 15 minutes, but finish at 325°F/165°C/gas 3 for 20 minutes.

White Rice Pilaf

- 1 cup/240 ml LOW-SODIUM CHICKEN BROTH (optional)
- 1 tbsp UNSALTED BUTTER
- 1 small or ½ medium ONION, cut into small dice
- KOSHER SALT
- 1 cup/85 g LONG-GRAIN WHITE RICE

The little black dress of carby accompaniments, rice pilaf is easier to make than you think. This recipe, in particular, will always yield great results. Use it as a side for sautés and chili or as a base for fried rice. I prefer a nonstick saucepan for less sticking and easier cleanup. If you don't use nonstick, just be sure to reduce your heat to super-low for the cooking; there'll be less sticking. Experiment with long-grain white rices to find what you like (my favorite is jasmati) and know that rices that cost a bit more often have superior flavor and texture. This recipe doubles easily.

SERVES 4 TO 6 AS A SIDE DISH

Fill a glass measure with the chicken broth (if using), and 3/4 cup/180 ml water (or 1 3/4 cups/420 ml water). In a 2-qt/2-L nonstick saucepan, melt the butter over medium-low heat. Add the onion and a pinch of salt, cover, and cook, stirring once or twice, until the onion is translucent, 6 to 7 minutes. Uncover, add the rice and 1/2 tsp salt and stir. Add the liquid, stir again, and bring to a boil. Cover with a tight-fitting lid and immediately reduce the heat to the lowest setting. Cook for 18 minutes, remove the pan from the heat, and let sit, covered, for 5 minutes. Uncover and fluff with a fork before serving.

Short-Grain Brown Rice

1 cup/200 g SHORT-GRAIN BROWN RICE

KOSHER SALT or SOY SAUCE

UNSALTED BUTTER or OLIVE OIL (optional)

I used to have trouble getting brown rice to cook consistently (there always seemed to be water left in the pan) until I tried this method, which a friend recommended. Basically, you cook the rice like pasta, and it comes out perfectly every time. I much prefer short-grain brown rice (plump, nutty kernels) to long-grain brown rice, so I am calling for it here. (Look for it in the natural-foods section of grocery stores or in bulk bins at health-food stores.) But this method works for long-grain brown rice, too. Be sure to use lots of water and a big pot, as you would for pasta, since the water will boil down, and the starch will cause the water to bubble up quite a bit, too. This rice is a great base for add-ins for both warm dishes and cool salads.

SERVES 4 TO 6 AS A SIDE DISH

Fill a pasta pot two-thirds full of water (at least 10 cups/2.4 L) and bring it to a boil. Rinse the rice in a fine-meshed colander or strainer and add it to the boiling water. Boil the rice for 30 minutes. (By boil, I mean boil, not simmer!) Drain the rice in a colander (reserving the pot), shake the colander a little to remove excess water, and return the rice to the pot off the heat. Cover the pot with a tight-fitting lid and let sit for 10 to 15 minutes. (The rice will absorb the remaining moisture.) Season with salt or soy sauce and add a bit of butter or olive oil if desired, before serving.

Cheater's 5-Minute Polenta

½ cup/120 ml **LIGHT** or **HEAVY CREAM**

1 cup/150 g **FINE CORNMEAL**

KOSHER SALT

2 tbsp **UNSALTED BUTTER**

⅓ cup/40 g grated **PARMIGIANO-REGGIANO** or **GRANA PADANO**

When I'm looking for a quick weeknight side dish, I make this fast and user-friendly polenta with fine cornmeal. (Generally, longer-cooking polentas use medium- or coarse-grain cornmeal.) This takes literally 5 minutes, and it's creamy, comforting, and the perfect pillow for a warm veggie sauté or ragoût. What makes this polenta especially easy is my favorite trick for preventing lumps: I whisk the cornmeal and liquids together while they're both still cold. You can do this ahead, too, and then cook right before serving. Polenta is best served warm, while it's soft and creamy; it firms up as it cools.

SERVES 4 TO 6 AS A SIDE DISH

1 ***In a large saucepan,*** combine the cream, 2½ cups/600 ml water, the cornmeal, and 1½ tsp salt. Whisk thoroughly before you turn the heat on! Turn the heat to medium-high and cook, stirring constantly, until the mixture starts to thicken and begins to bubble, about 4 minutes. Immediately reduce the heat to low and continue cooking, stirring constantly, until the polenta has thickened to a creamy, porridge-like consistency, about 1 minute more.

2 ***Remove the pan from the heat,*** and, using a silicone spatula or wooden spoon, stir in the butter and cheese. Taste and add more salt (if desired). Serve immediately by spooning into individual serving bowls or onto plates. (It will firm up quickly.)

TIP: Pour any leftover polenta into a small, buttered baking dish. Smooth out the top, cover with plastic wrap, and let cool. Refrigerate when cool. Gently reheat this firm polenta in the oven, or slice into pieces and pan-fry in butter.

How to Get the Best Results from a Recipe

Carpenters say, "Measure twice, cut once." I'm not sure there's an exact analogy in cooking, but the idea is to be absolutely sure you know what road you're going down before you start walking! Please, just read the directions thoroughly before you start to cook (twice if you can, but at least once all the way through!). My dear friend Polly (not her real name, but she knows who she is) set out to make what she thought were my quick-roasted plum tomatoes in *Fast, Fresh & Green*, but she was actually following the recipe for a slow-roasted heirloom-tomato gratin, which takes 2 hours to cook in the oven. She doesn't like to read headnotes; she's a dive-in type. And I'm afraid she's not alone. Please read the headnotes, if you can bear it. There's likely something valuable buried in all those words.

Then, like a carpenter, measure carefully, not cavalierly. Until you are an expert at eyeballing (which few of us are), you will get the best results from these recipes by using liquid measures for liquid ingredients, dry measures for dry ingredients, and, ideally, a scale for many of those dry ingredients. For consistently good pizza dough and tart dough, you can't beat the accuracy of a scale. If you don't have one, measure the same way every time. Use a spoon to transfer flour lightly into cups. Don't drag the cup through the flour, as that compacts the flour. My standard weight for a cup of flour is 4.5 oz/130 g.

Get to know your oven, your stovetop, and your equipment. Most home ovens are not calibrated correctly, so if you have the opportunity, get yours professionally calibrated. If not buy one or two oven thermometers and double-check the temperature of your oven at different heat levels. If it runs 25°F/15°C hot or cool, adjust accordingly. Likewise, for stovetop cooking, pay attention to sensual clues and doneness tests in the recipes to gauge if your medium or medium-high is in line with what the recipe says should be happening. If not, don't be afraid to raise or reduce the temperature. Finally, whenever possible, use the exact size and type of pan called for in a recipe. If you are not getting the results you want from a lightweight pan—or one that has dimensions different from those a recipe calls for—consider upgrading. You won't be sorry when you see and taste the great results you'll get.

How to Slice, Dice, Chop & Process Tricky Ingredients

There are some ingredients that I use over and over in making delicious veggie dishes, so I've developed favorite ways to prep them. Follow these tips, and you'll find that prep goes faster and that flavor and texture get better.

Make fresh bread crumbs in a coffee grinder. I keep a little coffee grinder in my kitchen just for cooking prep, and I love to whiz bread in it to make fresh bread crumbs. Sometimes I use the end of old sandwich loaves (which I keep in the freezer with most of my bread), but I'm especially fond of using English muffins for bread crumbs, as I love their texture. It takes two seconds to whiz one in the coffee grinder (to keep the crumbs coarse, don't overwhiz), and in no time I've fresh crumbs for a gratin or pasta topping. I never buy those dry, powdery bread crumbs in a can, nor do I use really stale bread for bread crumbs. Day old is fine, but rock-hard bread will turn to dust. If I've got a lot of bread to use up and a little more time, I'll use my food processor instead of my coffee grinder. Then (oh, joy!) I've got a big batch of crumbs to pop into the freezer (they'll keep well for a month) and to grab at a moment's notice. They defrost in minutes and are still "fresh."

Use the chopping blade of your food processor to grate Parmigiano. I know, I know—I use a lot of Parmigiano-Reggiano in this book. It's simply my favorite cheese, and its nutty flavor is an absolute match with many vegetables. Please do not buy preground Parmesan at the grocery unless you are absolutely positive—the wheel of Reggiano is sitting right there—that it is Parmigiano-Reggiano and has been recently grated. Anything white and powdery and vaguely labeled is likely to ruin any dish you use it in. If you are trying to save money, as I often am, Grana Padano is an okay substitute. Good Grana and Reggiano will both have branded rinds, so check the rind for authenticity. Buy a small block, and choose one without a lot of rind to get your money's worth.

While I love finely grated Parmigiano for a light garnish, I prefer coarsely grated (or, rather, chopped) Parm for cooking. I especially like the pebbly texture I get from chopping Parm in my food processor—with the chopping blade, not the grating disk. I cut any rind off my block of cheese, cut the remainder into small pieces, and process the pieces until they are the size of small pebbles. I store the chopped cheese in a covered container in my fridge to use on pastas and pizzas, in gratins and salads, and sometimes for nibbling!

Use a very sharp knife for fresh herbs. Basil, mint, and parsley bruise easily, so choose your sharpest knife to chop them, and don't overchop, which can cause bitterness. Coarse pieces are fine for most recipes in this book, and thin slices are even better. If you have several mint or basil leaves to cut, stack them on top of each other, roll them up cigar-style, and cut the roll crosswise very thinly. This technique—called a chiffonade—will yield delicate, pretty ribbons of fresh herbs. Lastly, you can avoid chopping altogether by using small herb leaves if you have them (perhaps in your garden in summertime). They make lovely bright additions to salads and pizzas.

Cut corn safely by snapping it in half first. Cutting corn off the cob can be dangerous. Take my advice and snap a shucked ear in half first. Then stand one half up on end (with the flattest end down on the cutting board) and cut straight down with a sharp chef's knife to remove the kernels. Repeat with the other half.

Slice a piece off the bottom of a wobbly vegetable before slicing. Cutting a round vegetable such as a potato or a turnip into thin slices can be tricky. Use this method: Put the potato on the cutting board and cut a very thin sliver from one (long) side. Roll the potato over onto that cut side. Now, it won't be rolling around; it will sit flat and happy on the cutting board. Leave it in this position and proceed to cut through it crosswise to make your thin slices.

Acknowledgments

Understand first that I am grateful every day. Since I moved to Martha's Vineyard four years ago and began my new life as a food writer/vegetable grower/citizen of the rural world, I have to pinch myself constantly to make sure I'm not dreaming. The fact that I also get to write cookbooks (plural—this is my second already!) as part of my job on this planet is almost too much.

I have two very special people to thank for this opportunity: my agent, Sarah Jane Freymann, and my editor at Chronicle Books, Bill LeBlond. They are my green-light, go-Susie team, and their confidence in me fills me up.

When I wrote *Fast, Fresh & Green*, it was a time of transition in my life, and I called upon a vast circle of friends and family to help me create my first cookbook. This time, I had a very tight (and I mean tight) deadline, so the circle shrank to a small but vital group of people.

When *The Fresh & Green Table* got the thumbs-up, the first phone call I made was to Jessica Bard, professional cook, food stylist, recipe developer, and person extraordinaire. She cross-tested every recipe for *Fast, Fresh & Green* in her professional kitchen, and darned if I was going to do *The Fresh & Green Table* without her. I jumped for joy when Jessica said yes, and in no time, she was hard at work giving me the same great feedback again. A thousand thank-yous aren't enough for Jessica (and her family, Callum and Grace, too, for all the PDFs and photos!).

And this time, I gave myself a real treat: the chance to work with my best friend nearly every day (courtesy of cell phones and e-mail!). Eliza Peter deserves a huge cheer and many hugs for signing up on short notice to be my chief "citizen" tester and then delivering her feedback and test results at breakneck speed. I thought Eliza—who was a great cook before I even got started—had done everything a best friend could ever do for a person over the last forty-odd years, but I was wrong. This was above and beyond! Thanks, Lou. And many thanks to Chip, James, Nathalie, Katie, and Opti, too, for being such enthusiastic veggie consumers.

Here on the Vineyard I'm lucky to have good friends who are also incredible cooks, and they were always standing by to lend ingredients, advice, or their taste buds. Thank you to fellow cookbook author Cathy Walthers for cheering me on and fielding my queries. Thank you to Katherine Long for ancho chiles—and a whole lot of inspiration. Thank you to Kay Goldstein for feeding me—and Roy. And thank you to Joannie Jenkinson, who isn't just a wonderful cook but also the most thoughtful friend a person could have.

Joining Joannie on the Vineyard support crew was my very dear friend Judy Fraser-Pearse and a small group of special women: Mary Wirtz, Sarah Saltonstall, and Renee Balter, who held my hand until deadline panic subsided. And very special thanks go to Dawn Braasch, owner of Bunch of Grapes bookstore; Liz Packer, owner of SBS; The Grain Store; and Jim and Debbie Athearn of Morning Glory Farm for all their support, too. I wish I had room to thank every individual in the Vineyard's amazing food and farming community, but there are simply (and fortunately!) just too many of them.

I continue to be so lucky to have my circle of *Fine Cooking* magazine experts (and longtime friends) to call on and work with. Thank you to everyone, but especially to Tony Rosenfeld, Sarah Jay, Martha Holmberg, Rebecca

Freedman, Jennifer Armentrout, and Mary Ellen Driscoll for being the special people you are. I'd also like to thank the loyal readers of my blog, SixBurnerSue.com, for your enthusiasm.

I'm especially grateful to have the chance to work again with the amazing team at Chronicle Books, and I thank every single one of them not just for their creativity and professionalism but for their good humor, too! (This is pretty darn fun, after all.) Sarah Billingsley is my heroine, but a big thanks also goes to Lorena Jones, Peter Perez, David Hawk, Amy Treadwell, Kate Willsky, Doug Ogan, Tera Killip, and Alice Chau.

And to my copy editors, the amazing food-smith Li Agen and Brenda Goldberg, many, many thanks for your swift and elegant editing of my many mouthfuls.

For abiding patience and love, I have to thank my mom and dad, Pauletta and Bob Evans, and my sister (and fashion consultant) Eleanor Evans. Thanks for putting up with the deadline disappearances. (Same thing goes for you, my dear friends Katie Hutchison, Chris Hufstader, and Liz Gray.)

But the person who should really be sainted for extreme patience, understanding, unconditional love—and grocery store runs—is my partner, Roy Riley. I don't have words (he'll be shocked at that, as I've been accused of chirpling more than our pet lovebird) to thank him for everything he does for me every day, not just deadline days. Mostly, I'm grateful for all the fun we have and for the gift of the bright and shining little star he brought into my life: Libby Riley. Libby and Roy, let's make pizza tonight—and every Saturday night.

Index

C

Q

R

S

T

V

W

Z